• HALSGROVE DISCOVER SERIES ➤

— DORSET'S —
HARDY COUNTRY

• HALSGROVE DISCOVER SERIES ➤

—— DORSET'S ——
HARDY COUNTRY

Rodney Legg

HALSGROVE

First published in Great Britain in 2003

Copyright © 2003 Rodney Legg

British Library Cataloguing-in-Publication Data
A CIP record for this title is available from the British Library

ISBN 1 84114 303 0

HALSGROVE

Halsgrove House
Lower Moor Way
Tiverton, Devon EX16 6SS
Tel: 01884 243242
Fax:01884 243325
email: sales@halsgrove.com
website: www.halsgrove.com

Printed by D'Auria Industrie Grafiche Spa, Italy

CONTENTS

*This book is dedicated to Canon Edward Brooks of Fordington Vicarage
who was the first to ask me to write about Hardy.*

INTRODUCTION

Writing about Hardy is exhilarating and exhausting. The first thing you realise from the extent of his work, and many feet of shelf-space devoted to subsequent biographies, is that he was an obsessively busy word-smith. That he won through, from a straw-roofed, working-class background, was owing on the one hand to perseverance, and on the other to his initiative in developing new plots and subject matter in an evolutionary process, rather than producing more of the same as his editors demanded. That would have secured his nineteenth-century financial security but not the enduring status of a world-class author. Having received the Order of Merit, and a visit by the Prince of Wales, he secured the admiration of the next generation of poets and novelists. He was never destined to be a great architect but he remains the only major British writer to design and build the house in which he wrote most of his work.

Hardy, having shaved off his beard, turned from novelist into poet

My aim has been to revisit the Dorset heartland of Hardy's Wessex as if with the author on a pre-car age exploration of its paths and byways. As with Hardy my first visits were usually by bicycle. In many cases his chosen places overlap my own, both on the ground in Dorset and away, with the coincidence that I also had grandparents living near Reading, and went through brief flirtations with London life and work. Wareham and its branch of the Hardy family are my roots, although the accident of a Bournemouth birth tends to spoil the credentials.

Thomas Hardy gives all the right reasons for returning home. His literary locations were told to Hermann Lea and have been added to by James Stevens Cox – some personally after he ordered a 'steak, rare, with a block of ice-cream', as was his somewhat eccentric gourmet habit – and authors Denys Kay-Robinson and Fred Pitfield. Personal revisions plus another score, several since recycled by other authors, have been my contribution to the game. Some 500 are listed in a glossary after the main text.

This book had its origins in visits to Canon Edward Brooks at Fordington Vicarage. Having asked me to write a feature for the *Official Handbook of the Thomas Hardy Festival*, in 1968, he later passed on his own anecdotes. The best, which I shall put into its 1907 context in the relevant chapter, concerns how Mrs Florence Hardy came to meet her husband: 'I was introduced to mine by Dracula!'

Some documents which belonged to the Moule family of Fordington, nearly a century earlier, were given to me by Tom Perrott of Bridport who chaired the Ghost Club in London. Roland Gant, who edited and published Hardy's revealing two-volume biography by Robert Gittings, sent me researching other possibilities. Eric and Anna Winchcombe, custodians of Hardy's Cottage birthplace, provided the counterblast to the opinions of Gant and Gittings, not to mention a barrage of bizarre theories from Lois Deacon who was sure that Hardy had fathered an illegitimate son by his cousin Tryphena Sparks. I left my mark on the living room by finding the old iron chimney-crooks that now hang in the fireplace at Hardy's birthplace.

Here I try to give a balanced view of Hardy and his relations, and a dispassionate reappraisal of his overlapping affairs with Emma and Florence. There is much more that could be written about Emma's dedication to the anti-vivisection cause, and Florence's later social work for Mill Street Housing Society. Not all you are going to read has come from published biographies. Here be other ghosts.

One

MONUMENT TO THE OTHER THOMAS

Thomas Hardy, the novelist, was between four and six years old when a new landmark gradually arose on the western horizon. It was clearly visible from the window seat in his cottage bedroom at Higher Bockhampton as he grew up in Cherry Lane which was known locally as Veterans Alley. His neighbours were the old soldiers and sailors of the Napoleonic Wars that took place a generation earlier. The landmark, which would be likened to 'a factory chimney' by Sir Frederick Treves, was for Nelson's flag-captain at the Battle of Trafalgar of 'Kiss me, Hardy' fame. Their notable common ancestor was Thomas Hardye of Frampton who founded the Grammar School in South Street, Dorchester, in 1569.

Thomas Masterman Hardy has been immortalised by Horatio Nelson's dying words. These will inevitably attract correspondence, even now, because they always do. The Nelson Society, and just about all historians who have looked in detail at his life and times, agree that he did say those words. Mr Beatty, the *Victory*'s surgeon, and Dr Scott, the chaplain, both confirmed that Nelson said 'Kiss me, Hardy' as he died in his arms on HMS *Victory*.

However, as at least a dozen correspondents are now in the process of telling the author, revisionist Victorians insist that the words he actually used were 'Kismet, Hardy'. That accords with our received notions of traditional British reserve of how the nation's greatest naval hero should have phrased his

The Hardy Monument rose from the heather and gorse when novelist Thomas was a boy

Coastal view, looking across Weymouth's hinterland, to Portland

language. The problem is that the Turkish word for fate and destiny, which would then have been rendered as kismat in its original Arabic form, was not current in the western world until later in the nineteenth century. So, we have to come to terms with Nelson's words as human and moving, as Georgian society did at the time.

Lord Nelson's favourite captain and companion in battle became Vice Admiral Sir Thomas Masterman Hardy. The second son of Joseph Hardy, of Portesham, he was born at Kingston Russell House on 15 April 1769. He went from active service to the governorship of Greenwich Hospital, being appointed on 6 April 1834, where he did much to improve the lot of the 2000 naval pensioners who lived in the hospital and Royal Naval College. He died in the Second Sea Lord's house at Greenwich on 20 September 1839, and his coffin lay in the dining room before burial in Greenwich Mausoleum.

By 1843, there was a determination to provide a Dorset memorial, and the sum of £609 15s had been raised by the public subscription among the gentry to commemorate his distinguished life. It was decided to erect a Gothic column on Black Down. This commanding peak lies in the triangle between the Hardy family's homes, at Kingston Russell, Martinstown and Portesham, with an appropriately sweeping view over Weymouth and Portland to the shipping in the English Channel.

The monument was designed by Arthur Dyke-Troyte. Its first stone was laid in 1844 by Mrs Floyer, wife of John Floyer, MP for Dorset and High Sheriff of the county. The contract price to Mr Goddard, the builder, was £375 19s 6d; for opening quarries at Portesham and quarrying stone, £111 13s 3d; to Mr Glegg and Mr H. Barnes for submitting designs, £5 each; advertisements for donations, £33 10s 11d; for beer £6 1s 8d and £2 19s 8d for bread and cheese, for the workpeople on the occasion of laying the foundation stone.

The base of the tower is at 786 feet above the level of the sea, to an octagonal design which inclines inwards like the batter of a medieval castle – from a base which is 28 feet in diameter – into parallel sides with a flared top for the viewing platform. Here the building reaches 72 feet, making a total height of 858 feet. A circular staircase winds up the middle, around the central pillar, and is sparsely lit by narrow slit-windows. From its prominent position it may be seen in every direction, and in clear weather at a considerable distance, from Purbeck and the Isle of Wight eastwards and from Start Point and Dartmoor westward. It is also a conspicuous object to vessels passing up and down the English Channel, as well as to all the surrounding country.

In 1901, W. Hardy Manfield of Portesham House, representing the descendants of Vice Admiral Sir Thomas Hardy, leased the Hardy Monument to the new National Trust for Places of Historic Interest or Natural Beauty, which was founded in 1895. The landmark had been restored in 1900 as a result of initiatives largely funded by Colonel Robert Williams MP, whose country seat was Bridehead, in the delightful valley at Littlebredy. It was the Trust's first Dorset property – leasehold, that is – with the first freehold property being the Cerne Giant hill-figure.

Another hero was commemorated on the hilltop in 1920. A stone seat was erected on the seaward side of the Hardy Monument as a memorial to Major William Digby Oswald who was killed at the Somme, at the age of thirty-six, on 16 July 1916 by the shell-band from a British gun which fired prematurely. A 'soldier's soldier', Oswald had seen action behind enemy lines and was a veteran of the Boer War, Natal rebellion, and Zulu rising. He was buried at Dives Copse, near Bray, on the Somme, but his comrades decided upon an English memorial, overlooking the Weymouth countryside where he had met his wife, Catherine Yardley.

Scaffold-clad, for winter repairs by the National Trust, to make the tower safe

At sea, the Hardy name would have a distinguished war record, being carried by a 1936-built destroyer of 1505 tons which was commanded by Captain Bernard Warburton-Lee in a defiant action against German vessels at Narvik, Norway, on 10 April 1940. HMS *Hardy* was lost in a courageous action which won Warburton-Lee a posthumous Victoria Cross. *Nelson's Hardy and Hardy's Possum salute you*, read a tribute attached to the door of the Hardy Monument, 'Possum' being the local name for Portesham. Her replacement, commissioned in 1943, was the flagship of the Royal Navy's 26th Destroyer Flotilla. She was sunk by a German homing torpedo whilst escorting an Arctic convoy, towards northern Russia, on 30 January 1944. Forty men were lost. 'Captain D', sailing in her as commander of the flotilla, survived and would retire as Vice Admiral Sir Geoffrey Robson.

In 1938 the National Trust acquired the freehold of the Hardy Monument and purchased three-quarters of an acre of the hilltop. Colonel Sir Robert Williams provided a fund for maintenance. Its car park and the surrounding slopes are owned by the Duke family of Maiden Newton. This open expanse of windswept vegetation is designated by English Nature as a Site of Special Scientific Interest, for its clumps of heather, gorse and wild bilberries, on the acidic gravel soil which caps the underlying chalk.

It is truly the heart of Hardy Country. Explaining that to visitors has become ever harder as Thomas One is now totally eclipsed by Thomas Two. The latter was fascinated by astronomical spectacles and would be delighted that the Hardy Monument is now the choice venue for witnessing cosmic events. It offers the widest of dark skies, in theory, though the hill-fog of reality is often as opaque as the mists of fiction. For often the Hardy Monument is literally invisible and bears out a popular Dorchester saying that predicts the weather: 'If you can see it, it is going to rain – when you can't, then it's already raining.'

Two

CHILDHOOD AT BOCKHAMPTON

Our Thomas Hardy (1840–1928) came into the world in the cob-and-thatch cottage at Higher Bockhampton of a jobbing builder and his extended family. At his birth – in the central room upstairs, the parental bedroom – he appeared a frail little thing, whom the nurse feared was dying. His father was Thomas Hardy (1811–92) and his grandfather was Thomas Hardy (1778–1837). Their house had been built by great-grandfather John Hardy (1756–1822), in about 1800, on an acre of land at the end of a sandy lane, leased from the Morton Pitt family of Kingston Maurward, backing on to the heath that extended to Puddletown Beacon and Puddletown village. John's grandson, Thomas Hardy senior, made Jemima Hand (1813–1904) pregnant. She was a cook in domestic service.

The Rhododendron Mile across Puddletown Heath

They married at Melbury Osmond, near Yetminster, on 22 December 1839. Thomas Hardy junior was born on 2 June 1840 in Hardy's Cottage which is now opened to the public by the National Trust. Because he was a delicate baby, aunt Mary Hann came to live at Bockhampton, in the parish of Stinsford to the east of Dorchester, to help look after Thomas after his sister Mary was born. That was on 23 December 1841 and aunt Mary stayed until her marriage to John Antell of Puddletown in 1847. Thomas's paternal grandmother, Mary Head Hardy from Fawley, Berkshire, also lived in the modest creeper-clad

Garden view of Hardy's Cottage with upstairs windows being those of the birth-room (above door) *and young Thomas Hardy's bedroom* (right)

North-east corner of Hardy's Cottage, from Snail's Creep path, with visitors at the American monument (left)

The parents' central bedroom at Hardy's Cottage where Thomas was born on 4 June 1840

Hardy's bedroom, towards the southern end of Hardy's Cottage, with the window seat where Under the Greenwood Tree *was written*

The Lodge in Yellowham Wood provided the setting for Under the Greenwood Tree

The girls' northern bedroom at Hardy's Cottage

The living room downstairs in Hardy's Cottage

Plan of Hardy's Cottage birthplace

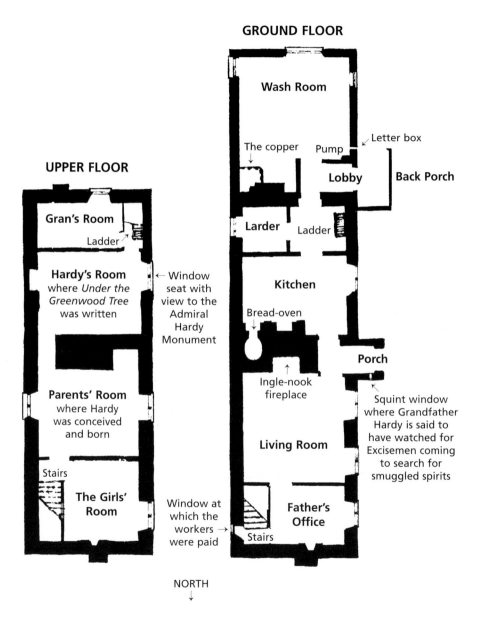

GROUND FLOOR

Wash Room

The copper

Pump

Letter box

Lobby

Back Porch

UPPER FLOOR

Gran's Room

Ladder

Larder

Ladder

Hardy's Room
where *Under the Greenwood Tree* was written

← Window seat with view to the Admiral Hardy Monument

Kitchen

Bread-oven

Parents' Room
where Hardy was conceived and born

Ingle-nook fireplace

Porch

Squint window where Grandfather Hardy is said to have watched for Excisemen coming to search for smuggled spirits

Stairs

Living Room

The Girls' Room

Window at which the workers → were paid

Father's Office

Stairs

NORTH
↓

building which Hardy memorably described as a 'a one-eyed blinkin' sort of place'. In a bedroom, Irene Cooper Willis tells us, there was the 'All-seeing Eye' of a portrait in oils of great-aunt Sarah Swetman from Tolpuddle, in her black widow's weeds of a generation earlier. Painted at the age of seventy-six in 1832, she was stern and brown-eyed with Thomas's hooked nose.

By the age of seven Thomas was not only reading serious books but played the accordion and could tune a fiddle. His father introduced him to country dance music and the hymns of Isaac Watt, which until 1842 he had played for the choir in St Michael's Parish Church, at Stinsford. Father and son played together at wedding receptions and country house dances. Over in Puddletown, aunt Martha Hann married George Brereton Sharpe, in 1841. An ex-Lancer, Sharpe became a farm manager for Lord Salisbury on the Hatfield Estate, and was to provide the model for Sergeant Francis Troy in *Far From the Madding Crowd*.

The piercing eye of great-aunt Sarah Swetman from Tolpuddle was a presence in the house

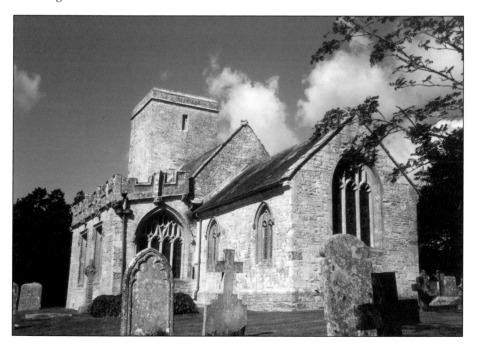

St Michael's Parish Church, no longer ivy-clad, from the south-east

Above: Stinsford House and the parish church in 1857
Above right: 'The big house' at Kingston Maurward
was the home of Mrs Julia Augusta Martin

The south front of Stinsford House before renovation

Thomas Hardy's formal education began in 1848 at the Church of England National School provided in Lower Bockhampton by landowner's wife Julia Augusta Martin from Kingston Maurward House. Childless herself, she adopted Thomas as her pet pupil, to the extent of cuddling and kissing him. Perhaps because of that, Thomas was removed to Isaac Glanfield Last's Nonconformist British School in the Greyhound Yard, Dorchester, in 1850. 'I can see 'en now,' an old man told Llewelyn Powys, 'a little nipper going off to school with a bag all a-coloured like Jacob's jacket.'

Here too Thomas was teacher's pet, being spared the usual discipline, because of his academic prowess. By 1852, as the family's building business was looking up after the Hungry Forties, Latin had been added to the school's curriculum, at an additional charge which the family could now afford to pay. Hardy devised his own visual recognition system for remembering genders, and had plenty of time for memorising as his average daily walk, to and from the centre of Dorchester, was 5 miles. When Isaac Last founded his own Academy in 1853, Thomas continued to be his star pupil.

By now the family at Bockhampton had grown, with brother Henry being born on 1 July 1851 and sister Katharine – known as Kate or Katie – following in 1856. Thomas continued to have his head in books and journals, on which he spent all his pocket-money, and shunned the company of other boys. In 1854 he had the first of his infatuations with an attractive girl, merely glimpsed on horseback, of the safe-sex kind that would transfer to actresses playing his *Tess of the d'Urbervilles* in later life. Another, red-haired game-keeper's daughter, Elizabeth Bishop, would be immortalised in the poem 'To Lizbie Browne'. Hardy's observations of young women also gave him many of the originals for characters in his novels. He confessed to 'immaturity' caused by 'lateness of development in virility'.

Things came to a head in his assault on elder cousin Rebecca Sparks, while both were drunk at a Christmas mummers' rehearsal in 1855, as a result of which he was told not to return to Puddletown. Headstrong Rebecca was quite capable of looking after herself and would prove that by marrying Frederick Paine and then leaving him immediately. The wedding ceremony finished with a blazing row and Rebecca walked out on Frederick as he stood

Humped bridge over an arm of the River Frome between Lower Bockhampton and the water-meadows

bewildered at the door of Puddletown church. As Hardy would observe, through Sergeant Troy in *Far From the Madding Crowd*: 'A ceremony before a priest doesn't make a marriage.'

The fifteenth-century church has survived, medieval and magnificent, complete with dark oak pews and a large gallery where musicians played at services until 1845. Puddletown and its volatile (and aptly named) Sparks family provided Hardy with the best of settings and stories. These were full of incident and emotion. Without the wealth of material that came from this working-class background – which he spent a lifetime concealing – he may well never have progressed beyond being a mere purveyor of plodding prose and pedantic poetry.

Hardy himself realised this when he admitted that Weatherbury folk were 'by no means uninteresting, intrinsically. If report spoke truly, they were as hardy, merry, thriving, wicked a set as any in the whole country.'

Three

ARCHITECT TURNS AUTHOR

Thomas Hardy senior worked for Dorchester architect John Hicks on the restoration of Woodsford Castle. Thomas junior was asked to help measure it for the plans and Hicks was impressed enough to offer him an apprenticeship; sixteen-year-old Thomas Hardy reported for work in the draughtsman's office at 39 South Street, Dorchester, in July 1856. This led to Hardy's first published work, a deadly dull press release for the local newspaper, describing the renovation of St Peter's Church, Dorchester, in 1856–57.

Woodsford Castle, measuring up of which in 1856 started the career of Thomas Hardy, architect

Right: Hardy's first published work was the press release for the renovation of St Peter's Church in Dorchester
Far right: Hardy's font, designed for Coombe Keynes parish church, is now at Wool

Martha Brown's crime of passion was committed at Birdsmoor Gate, Marshwood

He may also have contributed articles to the *Dorset County Chronicle* on similar projects at Rampisham, Powerstock, Bridport, Coombe Keynes and new Gothic churches provided for Athelhampton and Bettiscombe in 1862. Drawings for the font at Coombe Keynes – dated 8 April 1861 – show it is Hardy's work, though to see it you now have to visit Holy Rood Church at Wool, since the parish church at Coombe Keynes was declared redundant.

In Dorchester on 9 August 1856, Thomas had one of life's pivotal experiences which resonated through his work, and still preyed on his mind in old age. Martha Brown of Birdsmoor Gate, Marshwood, had found her husband, John, in the act of making love to Mary Davies. In the row that followed, John hit Martha with his carter's whip. She retaliated with a hatchet in the ultimate crime of passion – for which she was sentenced to death. The hanging was in public from the 'New Drop' over the low stone arch into the County Gaol in North Square, Dorchester. Hardy had one of the best views as a crowd of 4000 gathered to watch. Revd Henry Moule, vicar of Fordington, accompanied her to the scaffold because the prison chaplain, Dacre Clemetson, was too distraught to appear. Martha, however, maintained her composure. With delicate dignity, in a thin black gown in the damp morning air, her soft features became moulded by the drizzle into a marble-like stiffness, making an indelible impression on Thomas Hardy. The judicial death of Martha Brown stirred the imagination for what he turned into his series of Wessex tragedies. He also watched, through a telescope from Rainbarrows on the heath above Bockhampton, the execution of nineteen-year-old James Searle on 10 August 1858. He had killed Sarah Ann Guppy, a 'deformed and diminutive' young woman, in an unprovoked attack at Stoke Abbott.

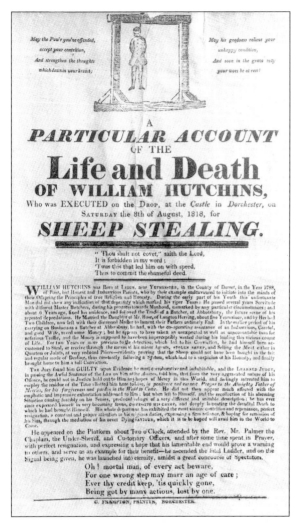

Public executions, witnessed as a teenager, had a lifelong impact on Hardy's writings

Revd Henry Moule, vicar of Fordington, accompanied Martha Brown to the scaffold

Hardy the architect, studious at twenty-one in 1861

Thomas's brother, Henry, was set to follow the family trade as a builder. Their sister Mary, several cousins, and other friends were dispersing in search of work. Emma Sparks, another of his Puddletown cousins, emigrated and died in Queensland. Favourite aunt Martha Sharpe suffered the same fate in Ontario. Fellow apprentice Henry Robert Bastow had gone to Tasmania. Another young acquaintance, Thomas William Hooper Tolbort, entered the Indian Civil Service. Their mutual friend and mentor, Horace, christened Horatio Moseley Moule – a brilliant but clinically depressed son of Fordington's vicar – urged Thomas Hardy to take the obvious next step in his chosen profession and make his fortune in the Empire's booming capital.

Hardy moved to London, into lodgings at 3 Clarence Place, Kilburn, on 17 April 1862. He had a return ticket, back to Dorchester Station, and made the rounds of architects looking for work. He might have had to use the ticket, had it not been for a chance remark, that Arthur Blomfield needed a young Gothic draughtsman to design churches and rectories. He was the son of a bishop, whose brother was also one, so ecclesiastical faculties were a family preoccupation. Hardy fitted the bill and reported to the drawing-office at 9 St Martin's Place, Trafalgar Square, on 5 May 1862. 'Any spice in the papers?' was Blomfield's customary morning greeting. Hardy fitted in well with his peers – 'Tory and Churchy' – and joined in their japes against radicals and reformers. Hardy's vision was backwards to Dorset rather than forward into the political future. Bar an abiding fascination in public executions, his notes and letters show hardly any interest in national or world events, but that applies to most young men in any era. On 21 November 1863 he accompanied Blomfield at the laying of the foundation stone by the Princess Royal at All Saints' Church in New Windsor. 'Take it, take it!' she said, handing the commemorative trowel back to Blomfield, having smeared her gloves with mortar.

In 1863, Blomfield's office moved to 8 Adelphi Terrace, overlooking the Thames from Adam Street in the Strand. Hardy lodged at 16 Westbourne Park Villas, Bayswater, near Paddington Station. His 'Essay on Coloured Bricks and Terra-cotta Architecture' won him a prize from the Institute of British Architects in 1863. 'How I Built Myself a House,' an article in *Chamber's Journal* on 18 March 1865, was Thomas Hardy's first paid work to be published. It earned him £3 15s – the average agricultural wages in Dorset for a month. On 27 October 1865, Arthur Blomfield with employees Hardy and Lee, attended the state funeral of Lord Palmerston, in Westminster Abbey. Blomfield, with his nose for gossip, would have been aware of the fact that Palmerston was the first British Prime Minister to die whilst making love to his mistress. This event took place on the billiard table.

Thomas Hardy was also enjoying an emotional fling, with Eliza Nicholls, whose father had served at Kimmeridge Coastguard Station. She was a maid to a barrister's wife at Westbourne Park Villas, the house in which Hardy had been lodging since the summer of 1863. When Eliza left for Findon, where her father was now stationed, Hardy moved on to an infatuation with her younger sister, Mary Jane Nicholls. That affair was over by the middle of 1867 when Hardy penned a poem of regret, 'Neutral Tones'. His health and mental state were suffering so he decided to return home to Dorchester to resume working for John Hicks who was also ill.

Back at Bockhampton he started work on his first novel in August 1867. The first draft of *The Poor Man and the Lady* was completed in January 1868. Hardy was applying all his spare time to writing – at the rate of twenty manuscript pages a week – with the physical result that he soon sported a beard. Though encouraged by publisher Alexander Macmillan and editor John Morley he withdrew the book while it was awaiting judgement from a second reader. It was then turned down by Frederick Chapman of Chapman & Hall, followed by William

Hardy's coastal diversion of the mid-1860s was to Kimmeridge Bay and its Clavell Tower with coastguard's daughter Eliza Nicholls

Tinsley of Tinsley Brothers, though the latter offered to reconsider if the author would pay towards publication.

Hicks died on 12 February 1869 and his work, together with Hardy, was taken over by George Crickmay of Weymouth. Work in progress included the rebuilding of Turnworth parish church for rich widow Julia Parry-Okeden in memory of her husband William. Hardy drew the tracery details of birds, leaves and flowers for the capitals on the columns, plus corbels of bearded heads and an owl. Mrs Parry-Okeden's home, Turnworth House, provided the original for Hintock House in *The Woodlanders*. The Dorchester drawing office was closed and Hardy worked from Weymouth where the office was at 77 St Thomas Street. He lodged at 3 Wooperton Street, a three-storey Victorian terrace house with a bay window overhanging the pavement, and a view over Radipole Lake towards the Hardy Monument.

Work at Turnworth parish church (centre left) *provided a prime rural location*

Turnworth House, the home of Mrs Julia Parry-Okeden, provided the original for Hintock House in The Woodlanders

Hardy threw his literary efforts into the melodrama *Desperate Remedies*, daring and erotic, which has the lady of Knapwater House in bed with her maid, perhaps because Hardy was thinking of the real-life house and owner, Kingston Maurward and Julia Martin, who used to cuddle him as a child. In a 'smouldering passion' the maid dresses her with 'silk stockings and white shoes'. Havelock Ellis, in his *Studies of the Psychology of Sex*, noted that Hardy showed 'an unusual but by no means predominant interest in the feet and shoes of his heroines'.

The *Dorset County Chronicle* of 28 October 1869 conveniently provided the description of a fire which devastated buildings at Athelhampton, which Hardy put to dramatic use. In February 1870, after cousin Tryphena Sparks – Triffie, with whom he may have been emotionally entangled – left Dorset for Stockwell Training College for Schoolmistresses in South London, Hardy quit his Weymouth lodgings and went home to Bockhampton. His sister Mary had also returned, after leaving college, via a teaching assignment at Dogbury Gate, Minterne Magna. She was now employed across the hill in Piddlehinton School. Younger sister Kate, at thirteen-years-old, would soon finish her schooling.

The final church commission inherited from John Hicks saw Hardy heading west in the early hours of 7 March 1870 – by foot and then trains – to Launceston, Cornwall. He went onwards by trap to St Juliot, near Boscastle, on the Atlantic coast. Here, that Monday evening, he was shown into the drawing-room at the Rectory, to be met by a blue-eyed blonde. 'Received by young lady in brown,' he wrote. She was twenty-nine-year-old Miss Emma Lavinia Gifford – born in Plymouth on 24 November 1840, she was only a few months younger than Thomas – whose elder sister, Helen Gifford, had married the widowed rector of St Juliot, Revd Caddell Holder. Hardy's expenses, refunded by Crickmay on 12 March, totalled £6 10s 9d. It was a fateful visit: one that was to bring him a wife.

As a writer, Emma's suitor had formidable hurdles to overcome in London's publishing establishment. *Desperate Remedies* was also rejected by Alexander Macmillan and John Morley. It was ruined, Morley wrote to Macmillan, 'by the disgusting and absurd outrage which is the key to its mystery – the violation of a young woman at an evening party, and the subsequent birth of a child'. Whether it was 'too abominable to be tolerated' we cannot say as the offending scene was removed at the insistence of the eventual publisher, William Tinsley, after his acceptance letter of 5 May 1870. He asked Hardy for a subsidy of £75 towards printing the first edition of 500 copies.

'A sweet face is a page of sadness to a man over thirty,' Hardy wrote on the eve of his birthday, adding sombrely, 'the raw material of a corpse'. On 16 May 1870 he had returned to Westbourne Park Villas – to work for Arthur Blomfield and also Raphael Brandon in Clement's Inn – although he retained the Cornish commission and returned there for a holiday with Emma in mid-August. He was back in Bockhampton a month later and as architect's clerk became the nation's latest anonymous author on 25 March 1871: 'Never will I forget the thrill that ran through me from head to foot when I held my first copy of *Desperate Remedies* in my hand.'

The Morning Post, in its brief mention, liked it, but the *Spectator* spoilt Hardy's hopes, at great length. Better reviews followed – with everyone liking the cider-making scene – but they came too late. Returning from St Juliot on 3 June 1871, after spending his birthday with Emma, Hardy suffered the ignominy of seeing his first book remaindered for half a crown by W.H. Smith at Exeter Station. Hardy returned to other work for Crickmay and took lodgings at 1 West Parade, Weymouth. He designed schools in Radipole and Broadwey, and the main cluster of villas around Greenhill at the northern end of Weymouth promenade. Bay windows and turrets came into vogue, as Belvedere-type watchtowers, so that the inhabitants could pretend to be mariners looking for their ships.

For Hardy, London called again in March 1872, and he lodged at 4 Celbridge Place, Westbourne Park. William Tinsley refunded him £60 from the sales of the book, and Hardy acted as draughtsman for Professor Thomas Roger Smith of the Royal Institute of British Architects who had the contract for Board Schools in the capital. Hardy then sold the copyright of *Under the Greenwood Tree* to Tinsley for £40 and his second novel was in print by June 1872. This time the critics were less hostile. Tinsley was no prude, having published titillating speculation on Queen Victoria and her Balmoral gillie, John Brown. He asked Hardy to produce his 'new story' in instalments for *Tinsley's Magazine*. *A Winning Tongue Had He* was accepted as a serial – starting in September 1872 – to be followed in book form by a first edition in three volumes, for £200. The title, however, was regarded as awkward.

In tribute to Emma it became *A Pair of Blue Eyes*. She stars as its short-lived heroine, vicar's daughter Elfride Swancourt, with Hardy himself being young architect Stephen Smith – 'pronounced moustache, and an incipient beard' – who comes to survey West Endelstow church. Rival in love Henry Knight is a composite of reviewer Horace Moule and a prophetic Hardy imagining himself as a writer in later life. His eyes have 'lost their boy-time brightness by a dozen years of hard reading' and now 'permeated rather than penetrated'. Away went Knight's pen, 'beating up and down like a ship in a storm,' with just ten minutes to spare, in order to catch the late post. The author had done just that in Cornwall, to correct the proofs for the first instalment, against a tight deadline in mid-August 1872. Thomas Hardy was no longer an architect.

Four

FAR FROM THE MADDING CROWD TO MARRIAGE

Proof that Hardy was winning admiration as an author came when the leading editor of the day, Leslie Stephen of the *Cornhill Magazine*, decided to poach William Tinsley's new writer. He wrote to Hardy with an offer he could not refuse: 'If you are, as I hope, writing anything more, I should be very glad to have the offer of it for our pages.'

Stephen followed this up with detailed advice on the plot for what we would call a soap opera. While not demanding 'a murder in every number' it was 'necessary to catch the attention of readers by some distinct and well-arranged plot'. Thomas realised the significance of the opportunity but for the time being he had to struggle at Bockhampton to finish *A Pair of Blue Eyes* for William Tinsley. Following it, he told Stephen, there would be a bucolic love story in which the principal love triangle would feature a lady farmer, her shepherd and a cavalry sergeant. Hardy promised to submit it to Stephen.

Hardy returned to London in June 1873 and visited Horace Moule in Queen's College, Cambridge. He returned to Bockhampton in July and the rest of the summer was spent writing *Far From the Madding Crowd*. Bathsheba Everdene and Gabriel Oak are based on Mrs Catherine Hawkins who, with bailiff Robert Spiller, farmed 525 acres around Waddon House at Portesham, with immense difficulty after the death of their shepherd, William Slade. Hardy apparently heard about them from his young cousin Tryphena Sparks who taught at the

British School in nearby Coryates, in 1868, and with whom he is alleged to have had an affair. The Puddletown of his youth, with his drunken wife-beating cousins, provided the basic setting and characters. Hardy's mother experienced dispossession and poverty in Melbury Osmond, where his aunt Martha had her fortune told, foretelling death in Canada. Her regimental husband in Hertfordshire – the prototype Francis Troy – and a tragic fourth man, bachelor farmer William Boldwood, completed the assemblage for the novel.

Hardy's fact-finding visit to Woodbury Hill Fair, crowded and joyful in a field enclosed by Iron Age earthworks above Bere Regis, coincided with the tragic death of his closest male friend and mentor, Horace Moule, in his rooms at Cambridge. The date, 21 September 1873, was a Sunday. Charles Moule had been summoned by telegram to come and comfort his brother. Horace was drunk and depressed, fearful that the self-destructive combination would cost him his job, and had withdrawn to bed. As Charles sat reading in the next room he heard a trickling sound. On entering the bedroom he found that

Hardy visited Woodbury Hill Fair, Bere Regis on a busy Sunday in September 1873

Horace had slit his throat with a razor. His last words were 'Easy to die' and 'Love to my mother.' Hardy also felt the family's terrible hurt and shared their feelings of guilt and rejection for the rest of his life. The effect was a general sharpening of his character writing, initially blighting Boldwood in his current book, followed by a grim tide of misery and misfortune that overwhelms all the main male characters in his future work and climaxes in the life and loss of Jude Fawley. Hardy's work abounds in unlikely coincidences but he now knew from personal experience that fact is more chaotic than fiction.

The manuscript benefited from Stephen's interventionist style of editing, with improvements and insertions, which also acted as schooling in sophistication and technique for Thomas. Judicious editing tightened the plot, deleting spurious conversations and observations, removing descriptions of rural eating habits, and took out pointless speculation about Sergeant Troy's apparent drowning. Stephen's radicalism offset Hardy's conservatism. He resisted the author's attempts at including lectures on self-improvement but had his own weakness in tending to succumb to letters of complaint about risqué sexuality. Stephen, a red-headed giant with a dog named Troy (purely coincidental), received corrected proofs from Thomas at his Kensington home, 22 Hyde Park Gate, in December 1873 and it started to appear, anonymously, in the *Cornhill Magazine* for January 1874. No one could question Stephen's place in the genetics of English literature. His first marriage was to Thackeray's younger daughter, Harriet Marion, and the second, to Julia Prinsep Duckworth, gave us Virginia Woolf.

Thomas went down to Cornwall to spend Christmas at St Juliot. He bought his copy of the *Cornhill Magazine* at Plymouth Station while returning to Dorchester on New Year's Eve. One surprise was that Stephen, always ahead of his time, had employed a female, Helen Paterson, as his illustrator. Another was that its reviewer in the *Spectator* identified another woman, George Eliot, as the author. Hardy failed to take that as a compliment and worried about becoming typecast as a yokel writer from rural roots. Class, or the lack of it, was an abiding obsession.

His own family were disappointed at its content and setting, seeing the bucolic scenes as holding them up to ridicule. They immediately realised that Casterbridge was the county town of Dorchester and Weatherbury the village of Puddletown. Identifying Hardy originals seldom requires much scholarship though he often moves the odd building or setting from one place to another or merges a couple of locations. Weatherbury Upper Farm (Bathsheba Everdene's inheritance) is based on Waterston House in the Piddle meadows west of Puddletown. Its Great Barn is modelled on the monastic one at Abbotsbury. Little Weatherbury Farm (tenanted by William Boldwood) is Druce Farm, between Puddletown and Waterston. Nest Cottage (Gabriel Oak's home, since demolished) stood beside the bend on Chine Hill between Druce and Waterston. Yalbury Hill (where Troy and Bathsheba see Fanny Robin) is Yellowham Hill on the north side of the present A35, with the original course of the road being a hollow in the trees between the 1992-built embankment of the dual-carriageway and the other tarred road beyond it. The milestone on Mellstock Hill (which Fanny Robin reaches) is the columnar Roman milestone on Stinsford Hill, resited in 1988 in the landscaping on the south-west side of the roundabout. The Buck's Head at Roy Town (where Joseph Poorgrass stops for a mug of ale) was in Troytown hamlet, the name of

Below: Puddletown, the home of Hardy's cousins, provided the setting for Weatherbury village
Below right: Tudor Cottage, in banded stone and flint, with a 1573 datestone, was the Puddletown home of broadcaster Ralph Wightman

The impressive south front of Waterston Manor, near Puddletown, which is inherited by Bathsheba

Monastic thatch of the Great Barn at Abbotsbury which provides the setting for Bathsheba's barn (in both book and film)

Above: *The Roman milestone on Stinsford Hill before being moved clear of modern roadworks*
Above right: *Druce Farm featured as Little Weatherbury Farm, tenanted by bachelor farmer William Boldwood*

which Hardy adopts for his 'wicked soldier-hero'. The 'little shop' close to Weatherbury church (passed by Bathsheba on an evening walk) was in the Palladian-style corner building in the Square at Puddletown. The gallery of the parish church, Weatherbury (where Gabriel is singing), appears as itself, being the intact 1635-dated gallery in St Mary's Church, Puddletown. Weatherbury Vicarage (visited by Gabriel) was at Dawney House, which was the old vicarage at Puddletown.

Pummery Fair, as it was locally known, was held inside the Iron Age banks of Poundbury Camp on the outskirts of Dorchester. Casterbridge Barracks are the former Artillery Barracks in Poundbury Road, Dorchester, which are now the county's Territorial Army Headquarters. Casterbridge Grammar School (attended by Francis Troy) was founded by a Hardy forebear, one Thomas Hardye, in 1569, on a site adjoining the south side of Napper's Mite in South Street, Dorchester. Grey's Bridge (over the River Frome) appears under its own name on the London Road into Dorchester. A chestnut avenue (used by

Fanny Robin to avoid Casterbridge) is Salisbury Walk on the almost flattened line of the Roman east wall of Dorchester. Casterbridge Union House (where Fanny is heading) is the Dorchester Union Poor Law Institution, known to all as the Workhouse, built in 1836 in Damer Road, Dorchester. The clock over South Street Almshouse (passed by Joseph Poorgrass on his way to the Workhouse) is that above Napper's Mite. The Corn Exchange (where Bathsheba faints in Boldwood's arms) appears as itself and is in North Square, Dorchester. Casterbridge Gaol (Boldwood in custody) is Dorchester Prison, also beside North Square. The White Horse Hotel, at the bottom of High East Street, appears as itself.

Further afield, Sherton Turnpike (where Gabriel catches up with Bathsheba) is West Hill Cottage, the turnpike cottage on the Longburton side of the junction of the A352 with the A3030, south of Sherborne. Budmouth Races (where Troy loses more than £100) is Weymouth Racecourse, which was on the edge of the marshlands at Lodmoor. Lulwind Cove (where Troy fakes his drowning) is Lulworth Cove. Greenhill Fair (Troy disguised as Dick Turpin) is Woodbury Hill Fair at Bere Regis. Kingsbere (through which sheep are driven) is Bere Regis.

Above left: The former 'little shop' on the corner of the Square in Puddletown
Above: Daisies, dandelions and cherry blossom complete the Puddletown setting

The result of the friction caused in the Dorset countryside by Hardy's characters and locations was that no member of his family attended the ceremony at St Peter's Church, Paddington, on 17 September 1874 in which Thomas Hardy married Emma Lavinia Gifford who had been staying with her younger brother, Walter Gifford, at 54 Chippenham Road, Westbourne Park. Thomas junior was the first and only of Jemima and Thomas Hardy's four children to marry.

Thomas and Emma headed south for their honeymoon, via Martin's Hotel in Queen's Road, Brighton, to Rouen and Paris, where they spent the rest of the month at the Hotel St Petersbourg in the Rue Caumartin. Emma's diary records that their visit to Notre Dame is followed by La Morgue, as if this is the most normal of holiday venues: 'Three bodies – middle one pink. Their clothes hanging above them. Not offensive but repulsive.'

The King's Arms, Dorchester, into which farmer William Boldwood carries Bathsheba after she has fainted in the Corn Exchange

Five

SWANAGE AND
THE HAND OF ETHELBERTA

Mr and Mrs Thomas Hardy arrived back in 'Dirty London' on Thursday 1 October 1874. After a few days of house-hunting, from the Freeman's Arms in Wimbledon, they moved into lodgings on 6 October, at St David's Villa, Hook Road, Surbiton. The reviews of *Far From the Madding Crowd* were largely favourable with the exception of that from Henry James in the *Nation*, New York, who found the only believable characters were 'the sheep and the dogs'. This was more than counterbalanced by *The Times* noting, of the human participants, that at least they were 'all working people' rather than 'the idle lords and ladies' of many novels. Hardy, however, was less than happy to be regarded as a working-class author. He also continued to anguish over the tendency for everyone to compare his country folk with those created by George Eliot.

The result, taking shape from December 1874 and bringing Hardy a £1250 deal, was that *The Hand of Ethelberta* would enter different territory. The Hutton brothers from the *Spectator* came out with the trite but timely advice that each book should be 'better than the last'. Emma encouraged Thomas to move on from the peasantry and their cows to Jane Austen's polite society. Below-stairs details came from the real lives of members of the Hardy, Hand (or Hann) and Sparks families and Thomas's flirtations with his cousins. The heroine, Miss Ethelberta Chickerel, takes her name from the village of Chickerell, near Weymouth. After all the angst and recriminations, the good news, in January

Hardy met Prime Minister Benjamin Disraeli to lobby for new copyright laws

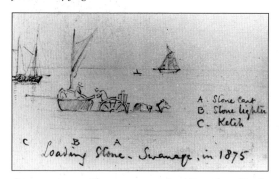

Swanage was still a stone port in 1875 when Hardy sketched the method of carting stone into the sea, to a lighter, which rowed it offshore to a London-bound ketch

1875, was that the first edition in book form of *Far From the Madding Crowd* was virtually out-of-print. One thousand copies had been printed.

In February 1875 the *Spectator* revealed its authorship – not by George Eliot, and not even by a woman – although the misconception persisted. On 19 March Thomas and Emma moved back to Paddington, to Newton Road, off Westbourne Grove. The following day, Thomas Hardy shared Leslie Stephen's disappointment as Cambridge were thrashed in the University Boat Race, by some nine lengths. Stephen also made Hardy his confidant, asking him to witness his renouncement of Holy Orders which formally closed an earlier chapter of his life. Hardy, meanwhile, was finding London increasingly expensive both financially and in its demands in social terms on the time needed for writing to deadlines. Everyone wanted to meet the successful new author. He had already shaken hands with the Prime Minister, Benjamin Disraeli, having joined a deputation of writers urging reform of the copyright laws.

Emma and Thomas took a train from Waterloo to Bournemouth on Monday 12 July 1875. They stayed for three nights in a guest-house and then took the steamer to Swanage Pier on 15 July. It was St Swithin's Day 'and the rain came down like silken strings'. An 'invalid captain of smacks and ketches', William Masters and his wife provided lodgings in West End Cottage, off Seymer Road. Bushes overhanging the path later featured in Hardy's posthumous collection of verse, *Winter Words*, in the poem entitled 'The Lodging House Fuchsias'. The coxswain of the first Swanage lifeboat, *Charlotte Mary*, William Masters ('Captain Flower' as Hardy names him), provided gruesome details of the way that 'the sea undresses' shipwreck victims 'leaving them naked'. He also explained the movements of double-tides. On 7 September, Thomas and Emma sailed around the Isle of Wight in the *Heather Bell* steamer (renamed by Hardy as the *Speedwell* in *The Hand of Ethelberta*), to see the 'spot where the *Royal George* went down' at Spithead. Emma tells us there were 'not so many masts as I expected'. They returned to their lodgings in the moon-light at high tide from Bournemouth to Swanage.

The replacement Swanage Pier (with its predecessor in the foreground) about to host the **Waverley** *paddle-steamer*

The scene in Swanage Bay, full of stone boats of varying types and sizes, painted by M. Croft in 1869 in a view south-eastwards to the stone quay and timber pier (right, centre) *and Peveril Point beyond*

In Hardy's time there was a fuchsia bush beside the porch at West End Cottage in Swanage

The return to Dorset enabled Thomas, belatedly, to introduce Emma to his family. Thomas and Emma set off from Swanage at 7am, 'packed as close as sardines' with fifteen fellow-travellers on Sommer's Van, plus another six picked up on the road. They arrived at Corfe Castle at 10.30 for breakfast and then a picnic with Thomas's sisters, Mary and Katie. The date was chosen so that Thomas could take notes on the third excursion of the newly formed Dorset Natural History and Antiquarian Field Club. Led by John Clavel Mansel-Pleydell, they arrived 'in a file of shining carriages' and were met by Thomas Bond, the local historian, who delivered the lecture in the castle ruins. Hardy incorporated the details, at length, into the new book and had Ethelberta attending.

It is with *Ethelberta* that the geography of Hardy's Wessex takes on regional completeness. Anglebury is Wareham where the Red Lion Hotel appears as itself. Sandbourne is Bournemouth. Wyndway House is Upton House between Poole and Lytchett Minster. Flychett is Lytchett. Rookington Park is Hurn Court (home of the Earl of Malmesbury, now Heron Court School) beside the River Stour between Christchurch and West Parley. Arrowthorne Lodge is Minstead Lodge, near the Rufus Stone, in the New Forest. Knollsea is Swanage (though it is Studland that has Knoll House Hotel and Little Sea). Hardy describes Knollsea as 'a seaside village lying snug within two headlands as between a finger and thumb'. Old Harry Rock, the famous chalk stack between the two bays, appears as itself, as does Nine Barrow Down in the Purbeck Hills. Corfe Castle becomes Corvsgate Castle (Corfe Gate being the ancient name for the gap in the hills) with the Castle Inn being itself, in East Street. Enckworth Court is Encombe House (home of the Earl of Eldon). Havenpool is Poole. Melchester is Salisbury. Solentsea is Southsea. London, Southampton and the French towns and cities appear under their real names.

Emma also took up writing at Swanage and produced *The Maid on the Shore*. Then the couple moved on. The final proofs of *Ethelberta* were sent from St Peter Street, Yeovil, in March 1876, for the book version sub-titled 'A Comedy

Wareham Quay and the town's ancient South Bridge into the Isle of Purbeck, as it was until the end of Hardy's life

of Errors', published in April by Smith, Elder & Company. It was an edition of 1000 copies. One was inscribed to Emma ('E.L. Hardy from the Author') but she never opened it, as was proved by uncut pages, when it was sold at auction in 1938. 'Too much about servants in it,' Emma was quoted as saying.

Though illustrated for the *Cornhill Magazine* by George Louis Palmella du Maurier, and promising so much, *The Hand of Ethelberta* failed to match the popularity of *Far From the Madding Crowd*. Hardy wanted to change direction again and suggested to Leslie Stephen that he should commission 'some tragic poems' as the next project. This was about the last thing Stephen wanted and it marked a parting of the ways though they remained friends. In May 1876, Thomas and Emma took temporary lodgings near Oxford Circus, in central London, and spent June touring the Rhineland and Belgium, where they visited the Waterloo battlefield, later returning to England from Antwerp.

Norman Churchill of Waddock Cross, between Affpuddle and Woodsford, typical of the war veterans from Waterloo to the Crimea whose stories inspired Hardy

Six

STURMINSTER NEWTON AND *THE RETURN OF THE NATIVE*

Cowslip time was spent house-hunting in the Blackmore Vale, followed by a holiday in Holland and on the Rhine, and then Thomas and Emma moved into their first furnished home in July 1876. The northern half of Riverside Villas, Sturminster Newton, was rented from Robert Young (1811–1908) and his family who lived nearby at The Hive, a three-storey house looking out across the River Stour from the ridge on the western side of the town. Young, a friend of parson-poet William Barnes

Below left: *Riverside Villas from the north-west showing the room* (top left) *in which* The Return of the Native *was written*
Below: *Hardy's pastoral view of the River Stour and Blackmore Vale from Riverside Villas*

Hardy's wine bill, paid by this £1 19s cheque to brewers Hall & Woodhouse, on 18 November 1876

(1800–86), called himself 'An Olde Dorset Songster' and published dialect verse under the pseudonym Rabin Hill. Hardy celebrated the view in his poem 'Overlooking the River Stour' and then proceeded to obstruct it with those most Victorian of trees, monkey-puzzles, planting one in front of each of the two villas. These led to confusion as to which half of the house the Hardys had lived in, as the southern monkey-puzzle outlived the northern one, but Hardy himself settled the matter when he returned to Sturminster with the Hardy Players in June 1921. They were entertained on the northern lawn by Mr and Mrs William Ponting. Hardy pointed up to the first-floor front room of their home. In his own hand he captioned a photograph of the same northern villa: 'House in which *The Return of the Native* was written – 1877.'

The countryman had returned to Dorset but not to his native heath. The lush green 'Vale of Little Dairies' around 'Stur' (as the market town is known) forms a landscape that is a world away from the heather and gorse moorland of Egdon Heath which stretched almost unbroken across the entirety of south

Dorset from the back wall of Hardy's birthplace to the marshlands of Poole Harbour. It formed a suitably prickly background to the interwoven marital relationships of the *Return* story which had been rejected by serial editor Leslie Stephen despite Hardy's acceptance of 'the irritating necessity of conforming to rules which in themselves have no virtue'. Stephen, for all his private radicalism, personified Puritan prudery in public. *Blackwood's Magazine* and George Bentley, for *Temple Bar* magazine, also rejected it. One wonders how any publisher could fail to see the commercial potential of the powerfully sombre opening, one of the finest evocations of landscape ever written, which nearly half a century later inspired Gustav Holst to produce his tone-poem 'Egdon Heath'.

Hardy's fourth approach was to Mary Braddon, the wife of Irish publisher John Maxwell, who edited *Belgravia* magazine. She liked what she saw but would only pay £20 for each of the 12 instalments, although George Smith of Smith, Elder agreed to publish the book version, in three volumes, with Henry Holt buying the American rights, to publish in New York a month later.

Above left: Colber Bridge, built in 1841, downstream from the bridge which carried the Somerset and Dorset Railway across the Stour
Above: Sturminster Castle, actually a fortified manor house, where Hardy made a nostalgic return for a theatrical performance of his work in June 1921

The story is set in the 1840s. Egdon Heath is the western extremity of the heaths between the Frome and Piddle valleys, extending 6 miles, from Black Heath at Stinsford eastwards to Throop Heath at Affpuddle. Rainbarrow, one of a group of three Bronze Age burial mounds, features as 'the pole and axis of this heathery world'. It survives on Duddle Heath, Puddletown, but is now overgrown with trees behind a tangle of rhododendrons. Mistover Knap is Green Hill to the south of Puddletown Beacon. Alderworth is Briantspuddle. The Devil's Bellows is Culpepper's Dish. Throope Corner is nearby at Throop Clump and Rimsmoor Pond appears as itself.

Tower of Affpuddle parish church, the East Egdon setting for the wedding in The Return of the Native

The Quiet Woman Inn was the Red Lion at Winfrith Newburgh – a thatched hostelry before being replaced by a modern road-house – and the name survives as the Silent Woman at Coldharbour, near Wareham. The latter, however, used to be known as the Angel Inn. The quiet woman, traditionally Anne Boleyn, was rendered silent on losing her head. The contemporary Quiet Woman Inn, in actuality, was at Halstock where the local legend is that she was a Saxon martyr.

Blooms-End, in the Frome meadows, is Bhompston Farm. Stickleford is Tincleton. East Egdon church, beside the River Piddle, is Affpuddle parish church. Shadwater is Woodsford and Shadwater Weir, on the River Frome, is at Woodsford and formerly had the 'ten huge hatches' described by Hardy.

As part of his researches, Hardy walked to Shroton Fair on 25 September 1876 and returned after dark across the Iron Age banks of Hambledon Hill, where he nearly got lost in the earthworks. He also attended the Toad Fair at Bagber Bridge, between Sturminster and Lydlinch, where a quack-doctor named Buckman provided freshly-cut toad legs in little bags which were hung around the neck as a cure for scrofula. The

shock effect of the twitching legs may have brought psychological benefits. The Hardys also attended concerts in the assembly rooms at the Swan Hotel in Sturminster. 'She is the sweetest of singers,' Hardy wrote, describing a young woman from Keinton Mandeville in Somerset. He was also charmed by a bullfinch near Cut Mill which trilled with 'a metallic sweetness piercing as a fife'. A man came most evenings from the town to the rise beside the house to watch the sunset. One winter afternoon 'the west was like some vast foundry where new worlds were being cast.'

Christmas 1876 was spent at Bockhampton though he never introduced Emma to the rougher elements of the family in Puddletown, or the cousins with whom he had been romantically involved. A reminder of his own exploits below stairs occurred one summer evening in 1877 after the Hardys' servant, Jane, returned from an excursion to Bournemouth with her boyfriend. In the early hours, Thomas spotted her emerging from the shed behind the house, with just a nightdress over her shoulders. The tall figure of a man loomed behind her. Emma reacted furiously, running downstairs and ordering the girl to bed, but by the morning Jane had disappeared. She had not gone back to her family's house and later it was found she had moved into her lover's home in Stalbridge.

The next news was that she was pregnant. 'Yet never a sign of one is there for us,' Hardy wrote, laconically, in his diary. It does at least imply that Thomas and Emma were still having a sexual relationship. Though the marriage was soon to come under strain, this turned out to be their 'happiest time' and Thomas summed up the period, in verse, as 'The Sturminster Newton Idyll'.

Seven

WEYMOUTH AND WIMBORNE

Thomas and Emma began to feel that Sturminster was professionally and socially out on a limb. Dorchester still seemed too close to home yet was also far away from friends and influence. *The Return of the Native* was appearing in the *New Monthly* in the United States but financial concerns made it imperative that new work was commissioned. They took the plunge and decided to give London another chance, moving into 172 Trinity Road on the corner of Brodrick Road at Upper Tooting on 22 March 1878. The Larches, it was called, at the end of three-storey Arundel Terrace, 'Beyond the Last Lamp' near Wandsworth Common. Here, in Hardy's words, their 'troubles began' with a distance and coolness coming between them. But despite a deteriorating relationship – exacerbated, it seems, by incessant wind and rain and sharing a persistent cold – they were still able to collaborate on preparing and copying manuscripts.

The publisher Revd Charles Kegan Paul (1828–1902), who had been vicar of Sturminster Marshall in Dorset until 1874, introduced Hardy to the Savile Club. Their social set included Walter Besant (novelist), George Bentley (editor), Robert Browning (poet), J.W. Comyns Carr (playwright), Sir Patrick Maccombaich Colquhoun (law writer and oarsman), Edmund Gosse (poet), William Dean Howells (American editor), Henry Irving (actor), Charles Godfrey Leland (American poet), Frederick Locker (poet), Joseph Knight (drama critic), Richard Monckton Milnes (1st Baron Houghton, poet and biographer), Walter Herries Pollock (author), Alexander Macmillan (publisher), William Minto (editor), Edward Henry Palmer (Orientalist), George Smith (publisher), and Alfred Tennyson (1st Baron Tennyson, poet).

In September 1878, back in Dorset to research *The Trumpet-Major* – a romance set in the Napoleonic Wars – Hardy called on dialect poet William Barnes at Came Rectory and dined with Reginald Bosworth Smith at West Stafford Rectory. London sources included the British Museum and pensioners at Chelsea Barracks. He returned to Dorchester on 1 February 1879 and was met at the South Station by brother Henry and horse Bob in the family's work-wagon. Back in London, his clique of fellow writers founded the Rabelais Club, having their inaugural dinner in the Tavistock Hotel, Tavistock Square, in December 1879. Professional jealousy, combined with homophobia, came to the fore as they took childish pleasure at turning down Henry James's application for membership. Ironically, years later he briefly joined Hardy as a holder of the Order of Merit, between New Year's Day 1916 and his death on 28 February that year. The poet Matthew Arnold called on Hardy in February 1880 and left him with the thought that 'energy is genius'.

Mowing the meadow on Pentridge Farm, across the river from Hinton St Mary, where William Barnes was born in 1800

In *The Trumpet-Major*, Overcombe is Sutton Poyntz, although its mill is nearby Upwey Mill. It was in 'an old woman's cottage near Overcombe' that Hardy saw a caricature of Napoleon 'as a maimed French eagle' hanging on a wall. He has his character Robert Loveday producing it from his pocket. Budmouth is Weymouth, and Gloucester Lodge, where King George III stayed on his annual visits from 1789 until 1805, appears as itself. It is now the Gloucester Hotel. Budmouth Barracks is the Red Barracks, above Hope Square, which is now Wellington Court. On the slopes around Bincombe the 'Grand Old Duke of York marched his men to the top of the hill, and marched them down again'. Oxwell is Poxwell. Springham is Warmwell.

The Royal Hotel on the nearby Esplanade, overlooking Weymouth sands

Leslie Stephen was the first to reject *The Trumpet-Major*. There is an anecdote to the effect that Stephen told Hardy: 'Heroines don't end up marrying the wrong men.' Hardy replied that in life they did so all the time. 'Yes,' was Stephen's riposte, 'but not in magazines!' The string of rejections also included *Macmillan's Magazine* and Blackwood's *Edinburgh Magazine*. Then came a lunch at the Savile with Revd Dr Donald Macleod (1831–1911), the editor of *Good Word*s, which lived up to its title with a commendation from the Society for Purity in Literature. Hardy was by now resigned, as he put it later, to moderating his prose 'in order to keep base [basic] life afloat'. The effect of Macleod's editing on Hardy's work was on the level of turning 'swearing' into 'profane noises' and making sure that dubious behaviour occurred on week-days rather than Sundays.

The next literary project was *A Laodicean*. Named for the infamous people of Laodicea in the Book of Revelation, it broke the Dorset rustic mould, and was therefore set around the more neutral landscape of Dunster Castle and Taunton in Somerset. Combining the erotic and intellectual it brought a generous offer of £100 per submission for a year's monthly instalments. These appeared in the new European edition of *Harper's Magazine* with George du Maurier as illustrator. Emma and Thomas went away in August 1880 for their summer holiday in Le Havre and Normandy. Hardy went alone to Weymouth and then Bockhampton in mid-September. The following month both Emma

Hardy, aged forty, in 1880

Bathing machines on Weymouth beach as Hardy knew it, with the royal arms having been carried by the one in the foreground

and Thomas visited three of the Moule brothers in Cambridge. Horace's suicide continued to prey on his mind and Hardy claimed to have seen Wordsworth's ghost. He was also disturbed to see the candles guttering into 'most fantastic shapes' which the superstitious country folk in his own family would have seen as foretelling a death. Hardy himself took this personally and expressed concern that he had made inadequate financial provision for Emma.

Much of that winter was spent at Tooting, in bed. He blamed it on an infection caught while swimming at Étretat. It seems more serious than that, with a haemorrhage causing him to pass blood, and then a stone from his bladder. For a time he feared the candles were right and he was dying. 'What a time I had of it,' he recalled. Emma not only nursed him but took dictation, for several months, to keep *A Laodicean* on schedule. Hardy was haunted by the recurrent dream of a multi-headed monster 'whose body had four million heads and eight million eyes'. He also blamed his poor health on London's damp and stagnant air and agreed with Emma that they had to return to Dorset as soon as possible. Wimborne, their chosen place, was the county's

Wimborne Station, opened in 1847 and closed in 1964, was Dorset's closest connection to the capital during Hardy's time in the town

major railway junction with lines radiating five ways, to Dorchester, Bath, Salisbury, Southampton and Poole. Before leaving the capital, Hardy, now able to use the pencil again, completed *A Laodicean* in April 1881.

On 25 June 1881, they spent their first night at Llanherne in The Avenue at Wimborne. It was an almost biblical experience. Released from London's murky sky into the clear country air, Emma and Thomas stood in the conservatory, thrilled by a clear view of Tebbutt's Comet. Hardy realised that the unexpected mystery object in the sky would be regarded at Bockhampton and Puddletown as an ill omen but for the new intellectual elite astronomy was widening natural horizons. Tebbutt's course was calculated with awesome confidence. No one on Earth is going to see it again until the fourth millennium. It set Hardy thinking about his next novel where he writes: 'That the magnificent comet of 1881 would not return again for thirty centuries had been quite a permanent regret for him.'

Llanherne, No. 16 Avenue Road in suburban Wimborne, with a blue plaque to commemorate Hardy's residence

'Lanhern' is the current spelling for the brick-built detached house which has become No. 16 Avenue Road. When the Hardys moved in, The Avenue was a gravel carriageway, and land towards Grove Road was a pasture. Hardy befriended land agent Robert Douglas whose brother was the Scottish author and landowner Sir George Douglas. Emma liked Sir George who encouraged them to holiday in Scotland. They visited Edinburgh and Loch Lomond in August 1881 and stayed with Sir George at Springwood Park, Kelso, in September 1891.

Thomas particularly enjoyed the company of retired county court judge Henry Tindal Atkinson whose daughter played for them on the piano at Berghmote. A younger friend, George Pike, lived in Grove Road from 1877 to 1894. George Lock was their hairdresser in the High Street. Hardy also befriended his physician, Dr George Batterbury, and allowed the town's Shakespearean

Society to meet at Llanherne. Local architect Walter John Fletcher often accompanied Hardy on country walks. Fletcher designed St John's Church, consecrated in 1876, to cater for the new residential district between Rowlands and Wimborne Station. The Society for the Protection of Ancient Buildings asked Thomas to keep it informed of any threats to Wimborne Minster. Hardy at Wimborne was as integrated into local society as he would ever be. Unlike Dorchester life, town gossip here was no threat, lacking problems of past associations and overlapping lives.

Wimborne Minster, hosting a performance of the musical Otter for Common Ground, *has been at the heart of Dorset culture since Saxon times*

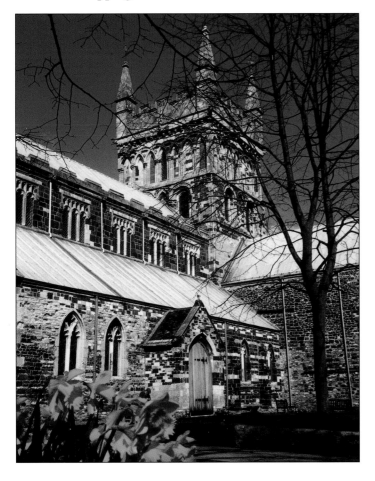

Hardy kept an eye on restoration work at Wimborne Minster for the Society for the Protection of Ancient Buildings

London and international publishers maintained their interest in Hardy. Short stories, such as 'Destiny and a Blue Coat' and 'Five Weeks In The Life Of An Heiress', appeared in the *New Quarterly Magazine* and Harper's *Weekly*. 'The Thieves Who Couldn't Help Sneezing' was published in a Christmas annual for children. Robert Buchanan commissioned 'The Impulsive Lady of Croome Castle' for his weekly magazine *Light*. Then Thomas Bailey Aldrich (1836–1907) signed him up for the *Atlantic Monthly*, to produce the much more substantial *Two on a Tower*, which Hardy began sketching out in November 1881. This was to be a scientific romance. Hardy wrote to the Astronomer Royal, to arrange a visit to Greenwich Observatory, on the pretext that he was considering fitting out a West Country tower to house a telescope. Writing began in earnest in the New Year. The procedure was 'lamentably hurried' and there was no time for proofs. Emma helped with the copying.

In December 1882 the orbit of Venus, goddess of love, put the planet directly between Earth and the sun, in a rare line-up next to be repeated in 2008. Eclipses had a particular appeal to Hardy who was fascinated by the immensity of inter-stellar space. Through 'Adonis-astronomer' and rector's son Swithin St Cleeve of *Two on a Tower*, he proves to be abreast of new knowledge – incorporating Harvard astronomer Edward Charles Pickering's work on variable stars – at a time when the universe was thought to comprise our one galaxy, whereas we are now told there are upwards of one hundred billion of them. All that before the next transit of Venus!

Hardy realised the competitive nature of scientific discovery: 'Publish it at once, in some paper, and nail your name to it, or somebody will seize the idea and appropriate it – forestall you in some way.' He also writes of sending off information in triplicate which was precisely what he was doing himself, with two copies of each chapter being posted to America – in case one was lost at sea – and the other destined for the book publisher in London. The conclusion to *Two on a Tower* is told in two arrestingly short sentences: 'Viviette was dead. The Bishop was avenged.'

For the location of Two on a Tower, *Hardy chose this monument in Charborough Park*

Right: *For the setting for* Two on a Tower, *Hardy placed it in the wood around this obelisk at Weatherby Castle, Milborne St Andrew*
Far right: *For the architecture of* Two on a Tower, *Hardy selected the memorial to Admiral Sir Samuel Hood at Butcome in Somerset*

Hardy's horizons were spreading again. Emma and Thomas escaped from the writing, 'playing truant' in Paris in October 1882, and on their return came to the conclusion that, as with Tooting, Wimborne was too close to its river. Thomas persuaded Emma that he needed to return to his roots, and they tried to acquire building land from the Ilchester Estate on Stinsford Hill, between Dorchester and Hardy's home village, though without success. The short story 'The Three Strangers' for *Longman's Magazine* in London and *Harper's Magazine* in Boston was followed by 'The Romantic Adventures of a Milkmaid' in *The Graphic*.

Wimborne and its countryside is woven into *Two on a Tower*, with Warborne as the Minster town. Welland House is Charborough House. As for the setting, its observatory tower is moved to Rings-Hill which is Wetherbury Castle hill-fort, at Milborne St Andrew. Rings-Hill Speer, a Tuscan column, is also

Victorian mortuary chapel and monuments in Wimborne cemetery

Wimborne in miniature at the Model Town

imported into the story. It is actually the Hood Monument between Compton Dundon and Butleigh in Somerset. Welland village is the hamlet of Almer near Sturminster Marshall. This makes the perfect example of a three-tier Hardy location. *Our Exploits at West Poley* was a boys' adventure story sub-titled 'A Tale of the Mendips'. There was also time at Wimborne to respond to a long-standing request for a 15,000-word factual article on 'The Dorsetshire Labourer' for *Longman's Magazine*. Published in July 1883, it made no mention of the most famous them – the six Tolpuddle Martyrs.

Eight

MAX GATE AND *THE MAYOR*

The first home in Dorchester for Thomas and Emma, at 7 Shire Hall Lane, has since been demolished for a forensic laboratory, with the name incorporated into Glyde Path Road. They moved in during June 1883 and stayed for two years. Hardy visited William Barnes at Came Rectory and walked with him to Winterborne Came parish church, beside Came House. The author had reverted to being an architect and was drawing the plans for a villa on the two-acre plot he had bought from the Duchy of Cornwall on the north side of the Wareham Road, opposite the former turnpike toll-house known as Mack's Gate which is under the course of the present A352. Max Gate was chosen as the name for their new home. To the east, below tree-covered Conquer Barrow and the ploughed-out bank of Mount Pleasant henge monument, is an 1835-dated marker stone: 'M B of the B of D' (Municipal Boundary of the Borough of Dorchester).

Hardy called on dialect poet William Barnes at Came Rectory, near Dorchester

The land cost £450 and the builders, the family firm of Hardy & Son, are said to have received a total of £1000. Income was also increasing, with £600 being offered by *Macmillan's Magazine* for *The Woodlanders* in twelve parts, which Hardy based around his mother's memories and countryside. Newspaper files were scoured for key moments and incidents for a story to be set around the county town and titled *The Mayor of Casterbridge*. He started on this in April 1884 and was also working on *Interlopers at the Knap* and *A Tryst at an Ancient Earthwork*.

Came Rectory, near Dorchester, where Hardy visited dialect poet William Barnes

Meanwhile the chalky ground at Max Gate was providing Hardy with his own collection of Roman-British antiquities. Clearance of the site took place in November 1883. Trenches for the foundations disturbed three burials in elliptical graves, cut into the bed-rock, with skeletons crouched in womb-like poses rather than being laid out. One had a bronze brooch at its head which probably fastened a shroud. Six black-ware pottery vessels were in a variety of tribal Durotrigic or imitation Roman shapes of the first century AD. There was also a splendid 22.5-centimetre-high cream-coloured ring-neck flask that had been made at the Corfe Mullen kilns at the time of Claudius, the emperor who undertook the AD43 invasion of Britain. More skeletons were found later. From the forehead of one Hardy took a pair of penannular-shaped brooches which had been joined by another early Roman fibula of the Maiden Castle class. Nearby there was a pit with the burnt bones of a horse and an iron spearhead. Covering one of the skeletons was a large sarsen stone which

Far left: Creation of the Dorset County Museum was supported by Hardy
Left: Dorchester's Roman defences, comprising a great earthen bank, at Colliton Walk above The Grove

Hardy had 'set up at Max Gate as a menhir'. Later finds, from the flower beds and vegetable garden, included decorated shards of top-class imported Samian pottery from later in the first century. Hardy quite rightly cherished his private collection of conquest-period native and Roman pottery, and other finds. They were kept in his private study, the contents of which went to Dorset County Museum, in 1936.

Excavations at Colliton Park, behind Wollaston House and below Poundbury Camp, have since gone some way to justify Hardy's claim that one can sense old Rome throughout the streets of the town. Howard Pell, in 1973, spent a couple of days showing this author hundreds of third-century Christian graves cut into the chalk that was being exposed by building work on the north-west side of the town. In all they must have numbered upwards of 2000. Then Chris Copson found remarkable evidence of earlier sacred monuments, built on an Avebury-like scale, during excavations before construction of the A35 bypass between

Above: *Replica Armada-period fire-bucket and the almost levelled Roman Wall* (left) *beside Salisbury Field, Dorchester*
Right: *Archaeologist Chris Copson with the Waitrose mural of the prehistoric sacred site that lay below its underground car park*

Roman floor in the Town House, Dorchester, with toga-togged Chris Copson explaining its underfloor heating system

the Trumpet Major public house and Hardy's garden wall at Max Gate. Their site is now an incongruous cutting which does nothing to enhance the literary setting as it cuts off the Hardy connections from the town. Similar prehistoric earthworks are depicted on a tiled mural beside the lifts to the Waitrose supermarket in Dorchester. Red circles on the floor of its underground car park show the site of holes for posts and stones. They confirm the prior significance of a town that is no Chester, Colchester or York but firmly belongs in the middle rank of Roman provincial centres.

West Dorset MP Oliver Letwin and folk singer Billy Bragg were among those appearing as Romans on the Dorchester hustings for the general election at the end of the next millennium. Hardy would have been delighted that 'old Rome' was back in town, if only for a day, and that a villa-sized Roman Town House is preserved in the shadow of County Hall. As a result of his influence, Lucia Catharine Stone, widow of County Treasurer Joseph Stone, preserved a

'fragment of Roman Wall' at Top o' Town, and presented it to 'the Mayor and Corporation of Dorchester' on New Year's Day in 1886.

Thomas Hardy took his brother, Henry, on holiday to the Channel Islands in August 1884. In 1885 Thomas found a wealthy new admirer in Lady Eveline Alicia Juliana Herbert, daughter of the 3rd Earl of Carnarvon, who married the 5th Earl of Portsmouth. Between them the two families owned 102,000 acres, including estates in Devon and Somerset, and might well have seduced the Hardys into moving westwards, were it not for the fact that the Max Gate project now anchored Thomas in Dorchester.

They moved into the new house on 29 June 1885. Hardy was far from happy, recording 'a fit of depression, as if enveloped by a leaden cloud'. The local surgeon, Frederic Bazley Fisher, attended to a recurrence of his Tooting bladder problem, but with only partial success. Friend and poet Edmund Gosse and

Above left: Section of Roman Wall at Top o' Town, Dorchester, given to the town by Lucia Catharine Stone in 1886
Above: Victorian plaque set in brickwork above the Roman Wall

Max Gate, south-east turret and conservatory from the front lawn

Below: *Drawing room and its view of the front lawn*
Below right: *The stairway*

Robert Louis Stevenson, a national celebrity since publication of *Treasure Island* in 1883, were among the first visitors to Max Gate. Mrs RLS, seldom lost for words, found Hardy to be 'a pale, gentle, frightened little man'. As for Emma, 'ugly is no word for it!' They called in August 1885 when RLS was living in Bournemouth and being treated for chronic tuberculosis. He was in the process of completing *Kidnapped* and *Dr Jekyll and Mr Hyde*. Thinking a change of air would ease his suffering, and choosing Dartmoor for the purpose, he stopped off en route for a few days at the King's Arms, High East Street, Dorchester. In the event, taken ill again, he never progressed beyond Exeter. 'He came out to my house unexpectedly,' Hardy recalled. 'He appeared in a velveteen jacket with one arm in a sling. He particularly wanted to see the room I wrote in, but as I had come into the house quite recently, I had not settled into any definitive writing place.'

Family life featured the first of a series of cats, Kiddleywinkempoops-Trot, and Moss was Hardy's labrador bitch. Their regular walk was a mile eastwards to Stafford House, which is now the home of *Gosford Park* scriptwriter Julian Fellowes and wife Emma Kitchener.

Extended visits were made by Lilian and Gordon Gifford, the children of Emma's brother Walter. Dorset's other well-known writer, parson William Barnes who was as old as the century, died on 7 October 1886 and Hardy wrote his obituary for the *Athenaeum*. He also gathered £400 in subscriptions for what took life-size form as the bronze statue by Roscoe Mullins, unveiled beside St Peter's Church in High West Street in February 1889.

Set back from the corner of Alington Avenue and Syward Road, Max Gate is an austere three-storey Victorian villa, much like those Hardy designed for Greenhill at Wareham, with rather squashed lines and a token turret. It was given its initial privacy by a brick wall, followed by a screen of hundreds of Austrian pines, behind which Hardy withdrew, though he accepted appointment as a justice of the peace. Both his sisters, Mary and Kate, were also back in Dorchester, teaching at the National School for Girls in Bell Street.

Robert Louis Stevenson, in August 1885, was one of the first visitors to Max Gate

Responding to criticism and playing to his strengths, in *The Mayor of Casterbridge*, Hardy created a strong and plausible combination of characters and plot. Leading participant Michael Henchard represented an amalgam of the powerful Henning and Trenchard families from Wolfeton Manor at Charminster. All the events and misfortunes, including wife-selling and a 'skimmity-ride' to shame moral outcasts, had their source in the files of the *Dorset County Chronicle*, now preserved in the library of Dorset County Museum. Robert Louis Stevenson was impressed and asked in May 1886 if he might dramatise the novel. Hardy accepted the offer but nothing materialised.

Few of the Dorchester locations are difficult to identify. The Antelope Hotel and King's Arms appear as themselves, as does the Three Mariners hostelry further down the north side of High East Street. The latter was an Elizabethan building, since replaced by a Victorian public house, and now redeveloped. High Place Hall is Colliton House in the grounds of which

Right: Shire Hall and its plaque (above) *to the Tolpuddle Martyrs who were convicted here in 1834*
Far right: Barclays Bank in South Street, Dorchester, with a plaque recording its place in fiction

County Hall was built in the 1930s. Barclays Bank, on the east side of South Street, has a blue plaque proclaiming itself as Michael Henchard's home. Court House is Shire Hall in High West Street. The Market House is the Corn Exchange in North Square. The adjoining Town Hall is itself, built in 1792, though replaced by the present Town Hall in 1848. Priory Mill is the former Friary Mill. The High Street is High West Street. Corn Street is South Street and Cornhill. Back Street is Trinity Street. North-West Avenue is The Grove.

Above left: *High West Street from Top o' Town, Dorchester, in 1853*
Above: *Town Hall and turret, designed by Benjamin Ferrey in 1847, replaced the building Hardy described*

Genteel Fordington, around St George's Church

Fordington High Street, towards the artisan quarter of the county town

Chalk Walk is Colliton Walk. Bowling Walk is Bowling Alley Walk. West Walk is West Walks. Durnover is Fordington. Mixen Lane is Mill Street there, and Peter's Finger the King's Head, Mill Street, Fordington. The Ring is Maumbury Rings, the Roman amphitheatre, at the junction of Maumbury Road with Weymouth Road. Ten Hatches Weir is itself, though only five of the hatches survive on the River Frome upstream from Grey's Bridge. Mai Dun is Maiden Castle hill-fort. Cuckoo Lane is itself, between the main road and Higher Bockhampton.

Whereas Casterbridge is Hardy's home-town setting, the Hintocks of *The Woodlanders* is based around the delightful landscape of his mother's upbringing. Composite vignettes feature the woods on either side of Bubb Down Hill and High Stoy on the mixed soils between the Dorset Downs and the western edge of the Blackmore Vale. Great Hintock amalgamates his mother's home

Above left: Entrance and top-row views of the Roman amphitheatre at Maumbury Rings
Above: Ten Hatches on the River Frome, upstream from Grey's Bridge

Multiple Iron Age ramparts, engineered for slingstone warfare, on the southern side of Maiden Castle

Above: *Bubb Down Hill, from old man's beard in a hedge by the railway, at the heart of the Hintocks*
Above right: *Church Farm, with the farm behind it, on the north side of Bubb Down at Stockwood*

Melbury Bubb comprises a church, house and farm

Hallowe'en pumpkin on the wall (left) *beside Manor Farm at Stockwood*

at Melbury Osmond and Minterne Magna where Hardy's elder sister started her teaching career. Little Hintock brings together settings at Stockwood and Hermitage. Hintock House is up on the downs, based on Turnworth House at Turnworth – where Hardy rebuilt the parish church – with Oakbury Fitzpiers the village of Okeford Fitzpaine in the vale to the north. The story coincides with Divorce Reform legislation in 1858. Fred Pitfield, in *Hardy's Wessex Locations,* explains that the topographical mixture may have come about to protect both the author and inhabitants from the risqué nature of the plot running counter to Victorian morals:

> *Hardy, in an attempt to avoid any possible allusions to real people, seems deliberately to have made some of the locations difficult to identify precisely – even some of the fictional characters encounter difficulty in finding Little Hintock.*

Marshcombe is Middlemarsh and Revellers' Inn the former Revels Inn at Lower Revels Farm, Buckland Newton, which was notorious for cudgel fighting on the outcome of which large sums were bet. This village appears as Newland Buckton. Tutcombe is Lewcombe, and Delborough is East Chelborough. The Earl of Wessex Hotel at Sherton Abbas is the former Digby Hotel in Digby Road which was rebuilt to coincide with the arrival of the railway line from Salisbury and London in 1860. It now accommodates The Digby dormitories of Sherborne School. Sheep Street in Sherborne is Cheap Street (with the latter deriving its name from the medieval word for a market).

The Woodlanders was finished on 4 February 1887, with Hardy noting down 8.20pm as the moment of achievement: 'Thought I should feel glad, but I do not particularly – though relieved.' The following month, when the volume appeared, he took Emma on holiday to Italy. While Hardy picked violets on John Keats's grave in Rome, *The Woodlanders* brought him a new offer, of £1000 from Tillotson & Son in Bolton for the serial rights to the next full-length novel. That would be *Tess of the d'Urbervilles*. Such was the reaction to *The Woodlanders* that Edmund Gosse was sent out to scour London for a copy one Sunday in 1887. Robert Louis Stevenson wanted to take it on his final journey from England to America. From there he would continue to the Pacific, Sydney, and death in Samoa in 1894.

Nine

ON TO *TESS* AND *JUDE*

The summer of 1887 saw the celebrations for Queen Victoria's golden jubilee with Thomas and Emma joining in at the Savile Club. Hardy the social animal, amid lords, ladies and the literati, declared himself 'neither Tory or Radical' but 'an intrinsicalist'. In January 1888 he hit upon the idea of effectively copyrighting his Dorset-based Wessex – telling Sampson Low to call their cheap reprints of his titles 'the Wessex Novels' – pointing out that he was the first to use it in fiction 'and it would be a pity to lose the right to it for want of asserting it'.

The Withered Arm headed a new two-volume collection of short stories published by Macmillan in the spring. Other successful minor works, occasional articles, and royalties from popular reprints paid the living expenses at Max Gate, provided a holiday in Paris in May 1888, and rented lodgings at 5 Upper Phillimore Place, Kensington. Once again, London brought illness, variously described as 'one of the worst cold in the heads' and a 'rheumatic attack'. Ideas for the next two monumental works preoccupied Hardy's thoughts. These coalesced around the names of the new characters. The forename Angel, for Tess's husband, comes from Angel Grey on a family memorial in the north aisle of Stinsford church. Jude can also be found in a church, on a brass plaque at Frome St Quintin where Hardy's Swetman ancestors lived. The story of *Tess* took shape over the winter of 1887–88 and was developed in tandem with that of *Jude*.

Much of the background for *Tess* came from family anecdotes, many incorporated in detail, and in *Jude* the thwarted aspirations of Hardy himself are combined with the abiding memory of the horrific suicide of his close friend Horace Moule. Among miscellaneous Moule family documents in the author's collection there is the following undated and unattributed pencil note:

> *Eldest son Henry, Curator of the Museum. Clare family in* Tess of the d'Urbervilles *is Moule family. Horace like Angel Clare. He was the most powerful influence on Thomas Hardy. Horace was the pivot of Traphine's tragedy. She was forty years his junior. Horace eight years older than Thomas. In his early novels the heroes were architects. [In] 1870 Hardy met Miss Gifford and for two years from July '70 Hardy was estranged from Horace and Traphine. There's never a villain in Hardy, only victims.*

Tess, who Hardy admitted was based on a real person, came from close to home. His paternal grandmother, Mary Head, remembered precisely what she was doing when she was told of the guillotining of Marie Antoinette – ironing, with the pattern of the gown being etched on her mind – which must be a universal reaction to such shocks through the ages, from the demise of King Harold at Hastings and the execution of King Charles to the deaths of President Kennedy and Princess Diana. Hardy's grandmother had been a close companion to tragedy, with her father dying shortly before she was born on 30 October 1782, and her mother following in the spring of 1788.

Mary Head was seduced as a teenager, by John Reed, and gave birth to an illegitimate daughter, Georgiana Reed in 1796. A few months later she was committed to the House of Correction in Reading on a theft charge. An unlucky few in such a predicament found themselves hanged, and many more were transported to Australia, but her accusers spared her by failing to present their evidence in court on 25 April 1797. The age as given in the records is two years less than Mary's, but as Robert Gittings has pointed out, such errors are not unusual for orphans, and her presence in the Bridewell would explain how she came to hear shrieks 'under the lash' as documented in a Hardy poem. Mary Head left for domestic service in Dorset and was working locally when she became pregnant by Hardy's grandfather and married him in Puddletown on 19 December 1799.

Tess as a name, of which Hardy would have been aware, was that of the Royal Navy frigate which guarded Napoleon in exile on St Helena. She once lost eight seamen who were working in the rigging, in a lightning strike. Under the command of the novelist Captain Frederick Marryat, HMS *Tess* fought in the first Burmah War, in 1825, and went on to have a religious after-life, as a floating Mission to Seamen in George's Dock, Liverpool.

The working title for *Tess*, half-finished in September 1889, was 'Too Late Beloved'. At this stage there was no d'Urberville ancestry to link 'succulent' Tess Woodrow and 'handsome horsey dandy' Alec Hawneferne. Publisher William Tillotson was dismayed that the story of a seduced maiden would outrage his readers and cancelled the contract. Hardy, now reasonably secure financially and no longer prepared to rewrite to suit market forces, offered the manuscript to Edward Arnold of *Murray's Magazine*. He also felt that ladies should be able to go through life without being made aware of the tragedies brought about by 'immoral situations'. It went next to Mowbray Morris of *Macmillan's Magazine* who also recoiled from the sexuality and thought that Tess was not merely seduced but was portrayed as making herself available for seduction.

Hardy was now forced to bend in the face of continuing prudish pressure and it was a bowdlerised serial that eventually appeared. Hardy's triumph was to return to these chapters and restore, and reassemble for the book that followed, the story of the epic heroine of English literature. Delay had brought benefits, and the transformation of Tess Woodrow into Tess Durbeyfield brought to her misfortunes the poignancy of lost inheritance, plus an implied incestuous irony to new and worse abuses that she faced. No wonder editors and clergymen regarded Hardy as a scandalously subversive writer who was exposing the hypocrisy behind Victorian values. Tess, whatever the opinion leaders might think, was 'a pure woman'. Hers is a 'real existence' not only in the sense of having had living sources but also for consolidating Hardy's personal position by bringing him fame and fortune. He had produced an everlasting best-seller, received with both critical and fashionable acclaim, which propelled him into top society.

The settings for *Tess* cover the whole of Dorset. The background is the riches-to-rags real-life tale of the Turberville family whose former manor house at Bere Regis is now Court Green pasture opposite the Royal Oak Inn. Their other mansion, Woolbridge Manor beside the River Frome, survives but became absorbed into the Weld family's Lulworth Castle Estate. Land around Bere Regis went to the Drax family of Charborough Park. In Bere village the West Street hostelry is now the Drax Arms but the Turberville name predominates inside St John the Baptist Parish Church. There is a Turberville window, with stained glass featuring the arms of families connected by marriage, and a cluster of Turberville tombs and brasses. Below, in the south aisle, the floor slab of the Turberville vault records: 'The Door of the Sepulchre of the Ancient Family of the Turbervilles.'

The Royal Oak Inn at Bere Regis faces the site of the Turberville family mansion

The Tuberville window in the parish church at Bere Regis

Medieval Turberville tomb in Purbeck marble at Bere Regis

The parish church of St John the Baptist at Bere Regis

King's Mill and the River Stour at Marnhull

The Pure Drop of Tess's home village is The Crown at Marnhull

The story begins in Marlott, which is Marnhull, where Tess Cottage on Walton Elm Hill was known as Barton Cottage. It is now Tess Cottage. Rolliver's alehouse is probably the former Lamb Inn, now Old Lamb House, at Walton Elm Cross. The Pure Drop Inn is the Crown Inn. Other locations in the Valley of the Little Dairies – the Blackmore Vale – include Stourcastle for Sturminster Newton and Nuttlebury for Hazelbury Bryan where the Antelope Inn appears as itself. Above the vale, Shaston is the real-life name for Shaftesbury, being its contraction on turnpike milestones. Bulbarrow, Nettlecombe Tout and Hambledon Hill appear as themselves on the chalk escarpments. Owlscombe is Batcombe and the Cross-in-Hand, a Roman column used as a boundary marker on Batcombe Hill, is the Cross and Hand. A shepherd warns Tess: ''Tis a thing of ill-omen, Miss.' Flintcombe Ash is Plush, a downland hamlet, above Piddletrenthide. Stagfoot Lane is Hartfoot Lane at Lower Ansty where Lane Inn is the old Fox Inn, on the corner with Cothayes Drove, rather than the present Fox Inn at former Ansty Brewery. Trantridge is Pentridge, near Chaseborough, which is Cranborne. There the Flower-de-Luce is the Fleur-de-Lis.

Nuttlebury is Hazelbury Bryan

The Cross and Hand on Batcombe Down – ''Tis a thing of ill-omen,' Tess is told

The Antelope Inn at Hazelbury Bryan

Then-and-now glimpses of Flintcombe Ash which is the hamlet of Plush in a downland valley near Piddletrenthide

Westwards, Evershead is Evershot where Benvill Lane is almost itself (Benville Lane) and the Sow-and-Acorn is the Acorn Inn. The village also has its Tess Cottage. Emminster is Beaminster. Long Ash Lane is itself, now the A37, on the upland section of the Roman road between Dorchester and Ilchester. Crimmercrock Lane, taking its name from an ancient burial chamber, was Cromlech Crock Road and is now the A356 across Toller Down. Both roads are near Chalk-Newton which is Maiden Newton. Abbot's Cernel is Cerne Abbas.

Above: *Lion Gate, guarding the entrance to Melbury Park, at Evershot*
Left: *Tess Cottage at Evershot, on the corner of Back Lane above the churchyard, retains its rustic look*

In the Valley of the Great Dairies – beside the River Frome eastwards from Dorchester – Talbothayes Dairy is Lower Lewell Farm, east of West Stafford. This village, with the Wise Man Inn, appears as Lew Everard. Wellbridge is Wool and Wellbridge Manor is Woolbridge Manor. Kingsbere is Bere Regis and Green Hill is Woodbury Hill which was famous for its agricultural fair. Sandbourne is Bournemouth. Bramshurst Court is now Moyles Court School, near Ringwood. Stonehenge appears as itself, as does Wintoncester, almost, as Winton is from its Latin name and the signature of the Bishop of Winchester.

The Royal Oak at Cerne Abbas, a Hardy favourite, providing a pit-stop for riders

Lewell Mill, on the River Frome, at West Stafford

The Wise Man Inn at West Stafford

Lew Everard is West Stafford village

Water-meadows between West Stafford and Stinsford

Above left: *Jacobean Woolbridge Manor at Wool is the pivotal place in Tess's tragedy*
Above: *Medieval Wool Bridge, over the River Frome, beside Woolbridge Manor* (right)

Tess as the ultimate Hardy heroine has her male equivalent in Jude. Hardy had his originals in memories of Horace Moule from Fordington Vicarage and Hardy's Puddletown uncle, cobbler John Antell. The latter, self-taught in the classics, also succumbed to black moods and alcohol abuse, deteriorating into a violent drunkard. The companion of *Jude the Obscure*, taking shape in 1890, is Susan Florence Mary Bridehead. The Florence came from Florence Henniker, married daughter of Lord Houghton, Viceroy of Ireland. She was the subject of one of Hardy's unconsummated flirtations. Susan Mary Jeune was a mutual friend at Arlington Manor, Berkshire, where much of the story is set. Aspects of Sue Bridehead's character, Hardy admitted, were 'suggested by the death of a woman' in 1890. This may have been his closest cousin, teacher Mrs Tryphena Gale – née Sparks – at Topsham, Devon, on 11 May. John Antell's widow also died in 1890.

Georgian transportation threat, on Wool Bridge, with a 1668 date-stone (right)

Hardy took the decision to shave off his beard in March 1892 – though retaining a wide moustache – before sitting for his portrait by William Strang. He heard that his father, crippled with rheumatism, had taken to his bed on 27 April. Thomas Hardy senior held out until 20 July 1892, and was to be commemorated by a poem, 'On One Who Lived and Died Where He Was

Born'. His sister Mary was returning to Bockhampton from laying flowers on the grave on 17 September 1892, when Thomas and Emma passed in a carriage, just as Stinsford House burst into flames and 'the firelight now flickered' across the churchyard. On going back to London, on 12 October 1892 Hardy attended the funeral of the poet laureate, Alfred Lord Tennyson, in Westminster Abbey but found it 'less penetrating than a plain country interment'.

Thomas was currently writing the serial version of *The Well-Beloved*. Set on the Isle of Slingers, as Hardy named Portland – which was his 'Gibraltar of Wessex' – it features Jocelyn Pierston searching for female perfection across three generations of the same family. There is a twenty-year gap between the episodes in which he desires Avice Caro, then her daughter Ann Avice, and finally granddaughter Avice. Needless to say, this being a Hardy plot, each affair is destined to fail before marriage. These unattainable visions paralleled Hardy's personal quest for his ideal Tess. She continued to appear before him for the rest of his life. He saw Tess in a succession of dairymaids, shop assistants, stage actresses and travellers on the train. 'I used to see people now and then with a look of her,' he admitted to Virginia Woolf in later life.

Hardy shaved off his beard and sat for his portrait, by William Strang, in 1892

Portland appears as the Isle of Slingers in The Well-Beloved, *named for the ancient slingstone pebbles of the Chesil Beach* (centre)

Above left: *Romantic ruins on Portland's eastern cliffs, with Rufus Castle overlooking the site of medieval St Andrew's Church*

Above middle: *Verne Citadel fortress, cut off from the island by a great chasm, is now Portland Prison*

Above: *Portland juts out into the English Channel with the Pulpit Rock being Dorset's southern extremity*

Castletown Pier and Portland Harbour which was constructed over a period of several decades during Hardy's lifetime

*Hardy joined the madding crowd for educational
entertainment provided in Larmer Tree Grounds by
General Augustus Pitt-Rivers, and became an admirer
of the latter's daughter Agnes*

Hardy stayed at Aldeburgh with Edward Clodd over Whitsun in 1894. Fellow guest Grant Allen summed up the weekend with a couplet:

How late we tarried, slow and tardy
Yet loth to lose one tale from Hardy

It was as *Hearts Insurgent* that Jude's story appeared in *Harper's New Monthly*, in 1895, and captured younger readers for Hardy's work, including twenty-nine-year-old H.G. Wells. Another was Agnes Grove, married daughter of General Augustus Pitt-Rivers, who danced with Hardy in the Larmer Tree Grounds on 4 September. 'For Agnes' is his poem in her honour. A vivacious and 'voteless' globe-trotter she was a thoroughly modern woman. Michael Pitt-Rivers told the author that his grandmother once entered the drawing room at Rushmore House and found Agnes 'sprawled stark naked across the chaise-longue'. Agnes told her: 'You are now looking at the body of the most beautiful woman in the world.'

Tess was still winning hearts, being dramatised by Johnston Forbes-Robinson for the London stage, and promised to leading lady Mrs Patrick Campbell. The earlier novels, reprinted during the decade by Osgood, were also moving with the times. Revisions included explicit language with the heroine in *The Woodlanders* now being able to say: 'He's had you.' *Jude the Obscure* was written without Emma having her usual moderating influence and was going to offend her Protestant fundamentalism.

The reviewers, sadly, were more in tune with Emma Hardy than the avant-garde Agnes Grove. 'Jude the Obscene' the *Pall Mall Gazette* railed, denouncing 'dirt, drivel, and damnation'. *The World* in New York went for 'Hardy the Degenerate'. Even his friend Edmund Gosse described it as the most 'indecent' work of fiction he had ever read. 'Garbage' was the epithet of the Bishop of Wakefield who claimed to have consigned it to the hearth. 'Filth and defilement' said Wesleyan missionary Thomas Gunn Selby. To G.K. Chesterton, Hardy was 'a sort of village atheist, brooding and blaspheming

Tess, Hardy's epic heroine, as she was portrayed in a Victorian print

over the village idiot'. Months later, changing his club to the Athenaeum, Hardy still felt the social opprobrium. On the other hand, *Jude* was proving a decisive commercial success, selling 20,000 copies over the winter of 1895–96. J.M. Barrie set the novels into context by making a comparison with the popular writings of Richard Jefferies and concluding that Hardy 'knows the common as well as Mr Jefferies knew it; but he knows the inhabitants, as well as the common'.

Despite Hardy's rheumatism and Emma's shingles they set off with bicycles (his black 'Rover Cob' and her blue 'Grasshopper') for Dover and peddled across Flanders in October 1896. The book version of *The Well-Beloved* rounded off the output of major novels. Completed in December 1896, after painstaking tinkering with the beginning and end, it closed the second phase of his working life. On 2 March 1897, Tess stepped from the page and appeared abroad, rewritten for the New York stage by Lorimer Stoddard and played by the director's wife, Mrs Minnie Maddern Fiske.

Ten

HARDY THE POET

Having achieved financial security, with the reassurance of a lifetime of royalties that would continue to enjoy copyright protection for a further half-century, Hardy could at last write what he wanted. That was poetry. It had been his personal predilection for years, ever since he had pondered over advice from Coventry Patmore that this was the 'proper form of expression', but magazine editors would only pay well for serialised novels which were the soap operas of their day. Poetry, even in its Victorian heyday, was eclectic and esoteric, free to venture beyond conventional barriers to thought, provided it did so in code. Hardy realised the poetic irony of the medium: 'If Galileo had said it in verse that the world moved, the Inquisition might have let him alone.'

On the other hand, if Hardy had anywhere further to take the English novel it would see him crucified by reviewers and churchmen, branded as a pornographer and turned, with Emma as well, into a social pariah. Thomas Hardy the novelist was about to reinvent himself as Thomas Hardy the poet. His first great topographical poem, from 1896, is 'Wessex Heights'. As well as Bulbarrow Hill and Pilsdon Pen in Dorset it features Inkpen Beacon above Newbury and Wills Neck overlooking the Vale of Taunton Deane from the Quantock Hills.

In 1897, after visiting Queen Victoria's diamond jubilee event by day-trip from Basingstoke, Hardy took Emma to Lausanne and Zermatt, in the shadow of

Dorset's highest hill, Pilsdon Pen, rises to 908 feet, with the most western of the big hill-forts dominating the Marshwood Vale

the Matterhorn. They then visited Salisbury before returning to Dorset to take Rudyard Kipling on a cycling holiday that was intended to persuade the nation's other great poet to retire to the county. Hardy's cycling distances expanded in 1898 when he accompanied brother Henry on a visit to a cousin in Bristol. Major-General the Honourable Arthur Henniker-Major, husband of novelist Florence Henniker who features in Hardy's poems, called at Max Gate while on manoeuvres with Southern Command. *Wessex Poems*, which appeared in the autumn, was Hardy's first collection of verse. It included many love poems based on 'little fancies', but only a single one to Emma who was understandably offended.

Athelhampton Hall, Dorset's finest Tudor mansion, features in both the novels and poems

'I can scarcely think that love proper and enduring is in the nature of men,' Emma wrote to Miss Elspeth Thomson who married *The Wind in the Willows* author Kenneth Grahame. She cautioned that 'at fifty, a man's feelings too often take a new course altogether' and then makes it clear that she is writing from personal experience:

Eastern ideas of matrimony secretly pervade his thoughts, and he wearies of the most perfect and suitable wife chosen in earlier life. Of course he gets over it usually somehow, or hides it, or is lucky!

Emma concedes there may be the occasional happy marriage but thinks these are restricted to Christians 'if both are' – with the word 'both' underscored – making it clear that Emma is the Christian and Thomas a non-believer. She may not have entirely given up hope as she presented him with a new Bible as his birthday present in 1899. They were in London and Hardy went to Buckinghamshire to hear one of his leading ladies, in social terms, reciting Thomas Gray's 'Elegy' beside the poet's grave. She was the stunningly attractive Helena Zimmerman, fiancée of the Duke of Manchester, and the words had particular poignancy for Hardy as they had given him his first really successful book title: 'Far from the madding crowd's ignoble strife…'

Thomas and Emma were brought together by their pets, sharing the grief when Moss died after being beaten by a tramp, and were active members of the Anti-Vivisection Society. Hardy urged that there should be an international convention outlawing the use of horses in cavalry assaults and restricting their part in warfare to transporting soldiers and supplies. Emma was an effective polemicist, with frequent and strongly worded letters to the press, such as that in the *Daily Chronicle* of 8 September 1899, on the behaviour of Britons abroad who 'trailed our national reputation in the dirt' by attending a bullfight in Boulogne. American literary critic William Lyon Phelps visited Max Gate in the summer of 1900 and found Hardy catering for a crowd of cats from all over Dorchester, plus residents Markie, Snowdive, Pixie and Comfy.

The Hardys joined the English liberal backlash against the war in South Africa, making Thomas the new century's first war poet, and giving Emma a political platform, to point out: 'The Boers fight for homes and liberties – we fight for the Transvaal Funds, diamonds and gold'. Hardy also felt sympathy for the British fighters, and showed it by cycling to Southampton and back – a total distance of 100 miles – to wave goodbye to Dorset boys as they went up the

Above and right: *Sad Sedgemoor: the site of the last battle on English soil, in July 1685, where the Duke of Monmouth's rebel army came to grief in Bussex Rhyne, having its echoes in Hardy's poetry*

gangplank into a troopship. His powerful poem 'The Dead Drummer' – later retitled 'Drummer Hodge' – remained the best of its kind until a new generation wrote from first-hand experience on the Western Front. In 'The Souls of the Slain' the ghosts fly home from South Africa like migrating moths.

Emma weathered a storm of personal problems. She nursed her widowed sister, Helen, who was terminally ill with dementia in Lee-on-the-Solent, while her niece, Lilian Gifford, looked after Thomas at home. Nephew Gordon Gifford, also living at Max Gate, was sent out into the world to follow Hardy's first career and became an architect for London County Council. Helen died on 6 December 1900 and personified 'By the Century's Death-Bed' which we know as 'The Darkling Thrush'. *Poems of the Past and Presen*t did well, with its first edition eventually selling out, but initial and subsequent sales – only 500 copies had been printed – were only a fraction of those of the novels. Hardy was a poet but to his public he remained a novelist. London's literary Whitefriars Club visited Max Gate in May 1901 to pay homage. War

Portrait of Thomas Hardy the poet

Portrait of Thomas Hardy, Order of Merit, in his Max Gate garden

continued to stir his mind but it had to be the conflict he heard about in his childhood. As an epic poetic drama *The Dynasts* was safely rooted in the Napoleonic Wars of a century earlier.

Hardy's mother, Jemima, died aged ninety on Easter Sunday in 1904. The date was 3 April and she was buried at Stinsford a week later. The family group at the funeral was headed by sons Thomas and Henry and daughters Mary and Kate. Hardy, now sixty-three years old, had a shrinking physical presence with H.G. Wells and others expressing surprise that he was such a 'grey little man'. Like his mother he suffered rheumatoid arthritis and increasing deafness, although, according to publisher Newman Flower, in later life he enjoyed telephone conversations with those who phoned Dorchester 43. The biographer Arthur Christopher Benson gave a different impression, having tried to host a discussion between Henry James and Thomas Hardy, which failed when neither could hear him or each other. Not that he was reclusive, as was proved on 1 September 1905, when Emma hosted a garden party at Max Gate for 200 members of the Institute of Journalists.

Hardy's working life was being rounded off by an intellectual triumph which received almost all his attention between 1902 and 1907. It passed muster. Adventure writer Arthur Quiller-Couch was by no means alone in seeing in *The Dynasts* 'the grandest poetic structure planned and raised in England in our time'. Perhaps the strongest critic was his wife, who not only placed Bibles in the guest rooms of Max Gate but opened the pages for the recommended reading of the day. She can hardly have been impressed to be told by her husband that the 'local cult called Christianity' would not outlast the 'systems of the sun'.

Eleven

SECOND WIFE FLORENCE

The mystic writer Edward Clodd (1840–1930), a wealthy merchant banker with the London Joint-Stock Bank Limited from 1862 till 1915, lived at Aldeburgh on the Suffolk coast. Precisely the same age as Hardy, he must have wondered quite what was going through his old friend's mind in 1909 when he pleaded that a 'young friend and assistant' whom Clodd had been inveigled into taking out to dinner and the opera – for reasons to be explained – was now 'so very delicate' that she needed regular holidays at the seaside. The lady, less than half their age, was Florence Emily Dugdale (1879–1937), a teacher from Ealing, who was a struggling creative writer. Her lucky break seems to have come about in June 1907 when Hardy gave her a signed copy of his *Wessex Poems*. She was soon having her work edited and extended in Hardy's distinctive ponderous style.

Florence had a 'kind friend' in Dublin, the surgeon Sir Thornley Stoker (1845–1912), who gave her a typewriter. Three of his four brothers were active in London's intellectual society – namely the author Bram Stoker, Thomas Stoker who was the retired Chief Secretary of India's North-Western Province, and George Stoker who was principal physician at the London Throat Hospital. Canon Edward Brooks told the author over lunch in Fordington Vicarage in 1968 that he heard from an elderly parishioner that she had mentioned to Florence her abiding interest in how wives came to meet their husbands. 'I was introduced to mine by Dracula!' Florence replied.

She became Hardy's regular companion in London but Emma was kept in ignorance. Emma lived a separate life at Max Gate, behind the dormer windows of an attic boudoir, which was her 'sweet refuge and solace'. She went off alone to Calais for the autumn of 1908. There was strife between them but Emma could at least joke about it, telling Edmund Gosse that she beat her husband each morning, 'but only with a rolled-up copy of *The Times*'. Hardy was offered a knighthood by Prime Minister Asquith but turned it down, allegedly because of the social implications of the semi-detached couple being reunited as Sir Thomas and Lady Hardy.

He managed to carry off a potentially tragic farce worthy of one of his own novels, as guest of honour at Covent Garden Opera House on 14 July 1909 for Baron Emile Beaumont d'Erlanger's production of *Tess of the d'Urbervilles*. Both his wife and mistress turned up and Thomas had to attend to Emma, leaving Florence to be taken in hand by Edward Clodd. Emma knew Clodd but disliked him for having renounced Christianity. Thomas slipped off to see Florence at the intervals. In August 1909 they went on holiday together to Aldeburgh, followed by Ventnor in the Isle of Wight in March 1910, and then annual return visits to Aldeburgh.

Hardy eventually engineered a meeting between Emma and Florence, at the Lyceum Club, Piccadilly, in 1910, which went so well that Florence was invited to Max Gate. It was a very twentieth-century relationship, revolving around Florence's flat near Baker Street, in which seventy-year-old Hardy introduced Florence as his 'secretary-help' and researcher.

On 6 May 1910 the nation grieved when King Edward VII died of heart failure and was succeeded by George V. For Hardy it turned into a significant personal milestone as one of the new king's first decisions, in his personal gift, was to appoint Thomas to the Order of Merit. The offer to join its elite ranks came in a letter from the Prime Minister on 2 July, with the ceremony arranged for the 19th, but Emma was unable to share the honour as she had returned to Dorset in poor health. Thomas, Emma and Florence had their public moment

Hardy and Florence Dugdale, his second wife, contemplating the future on the beach at Aldeburgh

together later in the year with the presentation of the Freedom of the Borough of Dorchester. They were accompanied by the poet Henry Newbolt. Christmas 1910 was a happy one for Florence who was now secure in her position as heir-apparent.

Hardy published a series of macabre short stories in the *Fortnightly Review*, as 'Satires of Circumstance' in 1911, and a similar piece on 'Blue Kimmy: The Horse Stealer' – hanged at Ilchester Gaol on 25 April 1827 – which he passed off in the *Cornhill Magazine* as the work of 'F.E. Dugdale'. Emma asked Florence to type her manuscript of *The Maid on the Shore* – which was at least in her own words – but time was not on her side. Suffering chronic pain with gallstones, Emma employed fourteen-year-old Dolly Gale from Piddlehinton as her personal masseuse, and she only descended the three flights of stairs for dinner. The domestic staff noted that Thomas and Emma no longer spoke. Emma's only weekly outing was in a Bath chair, pushed by the gardener, to the Sunday morning service at St George's, Fordington. She did, however, take her poems, in a collection called 'Alleys' and a manic collection of apocalyptic religious effusions entitled 'Spaces', to the printers in Dorchester.

To mark Hardy's seventy-first birthday, on 2 June 1911, Henry Newbolt and W.B. Yeats visited Max Gate to present the gold medal of the Royal Society of Literature. Emma recovered enough to host the garden party and made a couple of visits to the sea at Osmington Mills and theatre at Weymouth. But the respite was temporary – and Emma was terrified of surgery.

An international tragedy, the *Titanic* disaster, intervened, and Hardy responded with a poem 'The Convergence of the Twain', published in the *Memorial Programme* on 14 May 1912. By the time that American admirer Rebekah Owen visited Max Gate, Emma was in agony, and in an even worse state when Dolly Gale went upstairs to the boudoir at 8pm on the evening of 28 November 1912. A few days before there had been a 'violent row' when Emma had made one of her rare visits to Hardy's room and 'saw the table littered with the remains of food'. They had hardly spoken since but now she was crying out for him. He hesitated in his reactions and by the time he had shuffled his papers and climbed to the attic she could no longer respond. 'Em, Em, don't you know me!' he said. Five minutes later she was dead.

Dr Benjamin William Gowring signed the death certificate, with impacted gallstones and a stomach ulcer being the stated cause, and Hardy sent a telegram to Florence. Emma's earlier collection – *Recollections* – survives but after the funeral Hardy discovered two other large manuscripts in her room. One was entitled 'The Pleasures of Heaven and the Pains of Hell'. The other was 'What I Think of My Husband'. Hardy read enough of them to realise the tragedy and implications of the contents. He sat in front of the fire into the night, slowly peeling off the pages, one by one, into the flames. Florence described them as 'those diabolical diaries' in a letter of March 1913.

By Christmas Florence Dugdale was in residence, dismissing housekeeper Florence Griffin, and also ousting Emma's niece, Lilian Gifford, who made the last of her regular visits. Hardy was remorseful with guilt in a long bereavement for Emma that spilled over into 'an expiation' of words, in a sequence of more than fifty poems during the next two years, expressing a passion he had denied to her in life. It was described by Newman Flower as a process of 'self-castigation'.

The world continued to shower honours on Hardy. Cambridge University bestowed an honorary literature doctorate and fellowship of Magdalene College. Mary Hardy realised that Hardy would have on his mind the memory of Horace Moule and his suicide there four decades before:

This is to congratulate you on the honour Cambridge has now conferred on you. It seems as if it came from that dear soul, whose dust, for so many years has been lying in Fordington churchyard.

In *A Changed Man*, Hardy featured Horace's father, Revd Henry Moule – Fordington's vicar for more than half a century – who was regarded as the saviour of his people for having publicly held Prince Albert and the Crown-owned Duchy of Cornwall to account for neglect of their duties as landlords, which had exacerbated Dorchester's cholera epidemic in the middle of the nineteenth century. With the loss of more old friends, and childhood loves, Hardy was paying his respects in verse to a growing army of ghosts.

Twelve

THE WIZARD OF WESSEX

Florence Emily Dugdale became the second Mrs Hardy in Enfield parish church at 8am on 10 February 1914, with the chosen hour 'being in keeping with the retiring disposition of the well-known author'. Only the priest and three others were present. Florence's father, headmaster of the nearby elementary school, gave away his daughter. The witnesses were Florence's sister Marjorie and Thomas's brother Henry. A wedding breakfast followed. after which Florence and Thomas took the train for Dorset just minutes before the press were alerted and twenty-six reporters headed for the Dugdale family home at 5 River Front, Enfield.

Hardy issued a statement carrying the myth that Florence had been Emma's friend. But even some of his close friends, such as Edmund Gosse, were surprised that they had never been introduced to 'my long-time secretary'. In penance for the white lie he undertook a trip to Cornwall in May to visit the Gifford tombs, but Henry Hardy felt too unwell for accompany him, and Florence reluctantly took his place, commenting afterwards: 'The whole process was melancholy.'

Worse was to come with 'such a sad, sad, book' of poems about Emma. The saving grace, bringing Hardy his greatest pleasure of these final years, was bought by Florence just months before the outbreak of the Great War. This was a Caesar terrier named Wessex. The two became inseparable and such was

Hardy's tolerance and laxness that he delighted in seeing the creature molest his guests, including the surgeon Sir Frederick Treves, and allowed it to eat from the table. Cynthia Asquith found herself having to 'contest' every forkful and something similar happened when the Hardys called on Lord and Lady Ilchester at Melbury House. Dinner had to be shared.

As well as making sure the postman came no further than the gate, he famously took a bite out of author John Galsworthy, and howled uncontrollably one evening in the presence of William Watkins, a Welshman, who founded the Society of Dorset Men in London. Hardy and Watkins searched the Max House grounds for an intruder. There was none, Newman Flower tells us, but for Hardy it was confirmation of what he had long believed. Wessex had mysterious powers and rightly sensed that something was wrong: 'Watkins left Max Gate at ten o'clock, returned to his hotel, and died two hours later in his sleep.'

Hardy was 'long obsessed by the incident' and joked to visitors who complained of feeling unwell that he could reassure them with some confidence that they were 'not yet in immediate need of Dr Gowring'. It was unknown for Hardy to laugh but he could chuckle as 'a happy smile would flick across his face like a flash of summer lightning'. Life revolved around Wessex and his fate became Florence's abiding nightmare. She feared 'the inevitable Wessex tragedy' in which the truculent creature was either run over by a car or seized by a policeman and put down before she could intervene and win a reprieve.

The primary medium of the new century was film. The first of Hardy's novels to make the transition was *Tess*, through a deal with Louis Vincent in 1911. This was passed on to motion picture producer Adolph Zukor (born 1873), who had founded the Famous Players Film Company in 1912 and, in 1913, arranged for cottage exteriors to be filmed in that far-flung part of Wessex known as New England, in the United States of America. Hardy made a day-trip by train for the trade showing at Pykes Cinematograph Theatre,

Cambridge Circus, London, on 21 October 1913. His reaction is unknown but according to Dorchester auctioneer and amateur actor H.A. Martin the film was 'grotesque', though his substantive critique centred on 'its interminable herd of cows'. Here he invoked professional knowledge: 'Even now, and much less frequently in the period of the novel, dairies of cows seldom exceed eighty.'

The next was to have been *Far From the Madding Crowd*, by portrait artist and film-maker Sir Hubert von Herkomer (1849–1914), who was sold the rights for £150. He died before production could start and Hardy struck a new deal with American producer Larry Trimble and actress Florence Turner in 1915. Trimble owned the Turner Film Company which established studios at Walton-on-Thames, Surrey.

Vintage thespian F.L. Lyndhurst, at the age of eighty-one, had established a glass-house studio beside the beach at Shoreham, Sussex. His protégés, the Progress Film Company, took on *The Mayor of Casterbridge* in February 1921. Producer and director Sidney Morgan visited Max Gate to discuss script corrections, particularly dialect 'titles' (the words of the silent films) with the author in April 1921, and also asked for advice on locations. These included Maiden Castle at dawn and the actors and crew arrived at the King's Arms Hotel at 1am on 2 July 1921. Fred Groves and Pauline Peters were Mr and Mrs Henchard. Fragments exist of the 'sold' wife meeting the Mayor in ancient earthworks, and of Elizabeth Jane and her lover beside Hangman's Cottage.

Hardy's own account, written in the third person under his wife's name, shows how Dorchester people took the filming in their stride:

> *Although the actors had their faces coloured yellow and were dressed in the fashion of eighty years earlier, Hardy observed, to his surprise, that the towns-people passed by on their ordinary affairs and seemed not to notice the strange spectacle, nor did any interest seem aroused when Hardy drove through the town with the actors to Maiden Castle, that ancient earthwork which formed the background to one part of the film.*

The first Hardy among the talkies was *Under the Greenwood Tree*, an adaptation with folk-songs as well as dialogue sound, though it would not be released until 1929, after the author was dead. *Far From the Madding Crowd*, the 1967 classic by John Schlesinger, starring Julie Christie, Alan Bates, Peter Finch and Terence Stamp, will probably remain an all-time perfect production, given that it used more Dorset and Wessex locations than all the other Hardy productions of the twentieth century put together. Few coincided with those in the book but that was inevitable given the extent to which Hardy's rural idyll had already been compromised.

Tess, starring Nastassja Kinski, would be refilmed after Roman Polanski paid the Selznick estate $25,000 for a reversion of the rights. For legal reasons it could not be filmed in countries that might enforce extradition proceedings, in relation to a case against him in the United States, and the Bagshot Beds geology of Brittany came up with unspoilt and appealingly rustic visions of the Dorset heaths as they would have looked a century earlier.

Jude, directed by Michael Winterbottom in 1996, was acclaimed for its 'visually remarkable adaptation' (though set in New Zealand and the Yorkshire Dales, not that much of Hardy's last novel takes place in Dorset). It starred Christopher Eccleston in the lead role, with Kate Winslet giving a 'mesmerising performance' as Sue, his vivacious cousin and illicit lover.

The other twentieth-century contribution to culture was war poetry. Hardy excelled at it, his natural depressive moods being fed by the carnage on the Western Front and the fear that the Kaiser would succeed where Napoleon had failed. For a time it seemed possible that the Germans might land on the Dorset coast. Hardy's poems have been seen as a protest against the war but are not the work of a pacifist. He deplored the truce in No Man's Land, supported conscription, and urged the 'crushing utterly' of Irish rebels.

Childless themselves, Thomas and Florence talked of finding a 'Hardy-born' heir – he was now the richest author in the country – and decided to adopt young barrister Frank George. The son of cousin Angelina Hardy from Puddletown and William George, landlord of the Royal Oak Inn in Bere Regis, he was born there on 5 December 1880. Called to the bar, on 17 November 1913, he was in rooms at Gray's Inn in The Temple and passed muster as 'the only decent relation'. Fate intervened in a horribly Hardyesque way. Sub-Lieutenant Frank William George of the 5th Battalion of the Dorsetshire Regiment fell in a bayonet attack on the Turkish front trench across the Valley of Death below Hetman Chair in the Gallipoli peninsula on 21 August 1915.

Thomas's beloved sister Mary also died, of emphysema, on 24 November 1915. Her failure to make a will put Thomas in control of probate as next-of-kin, causing a rift in the dysfunctional Hardy family, with brother Henry swearing at Thomas, and sister Kate reduced to moody silence. The discord marred the funeral and hardened the family's hostility to Florence who they feared would walk off with the author's riches. Hardy took refuge in his study, producing some of his most intense poems as a retreat into memory, and was now almost a recluse in Dorchester. 'My reminiscences; no, never!' he told Sir George Douglas in December 1915. Finding it agonising to read old letters and documents, he gathered odd thoughts for his poems, and then destroyed them: 'They raise ghosts.'

In the awful middle of the war, in September 1916, he took Florence on a visit from Emma's Plymouth birthplace to meet her Launceston cousins and see the monument he had designed in St Juliot Church. Florence, who was often unwell, confessed to 'home worries, of a kind to break down any woman's nerve'. This included strife with the domestic servants and the cook at Max Gate was often only minutes away from walking out. The Hardys also managed to engineer a totally unnecessary rift with their oldest and wealthiest mutual friend. They feared Edward Clodd's forthcoming *Memories* might disclose their secrets but in the event they were 'so dull' that nothing was revealed. It was doubly unfortunate that his place was taken by opportunistic Sydney Cockerell from the Fitzwilliam Museum at Cambridge who talked his way into becoming Hardy's literary executor. Hardy and

Florence experienced warfare at somewhat closer quarters by way of the 'little pop' of a Zeppelin air-raid on London from J.M. Barrie's flat.

Touchingly, on publication of *Moments of Vision*, Hardy inscribed the 'first copy of the first edition, to the first of women Florence Hardy'. It ends with the wonderful poem, 'Afterwards', in which Hardy writes his own obituary as 'a man who used to notice such things' with memorable images such as the hedgehog furtively crossing the lawn.

Hardy's eightieth birthday in 1920, bringing 200 congratulatory telegrams, prompted Florence to mount a campaign to persuade Thomas to modernise Max Gate. It was no longer acceptable, she argued, for it to be the only big house in Dorchester without a bathroom. Well-pumped water was still being heated in saucepans in front of the fire and poured into a hip-bath. Thomas was in the running for the Nobel Prize for Literature but had to be satisfied with an honorary D.Lit from Oxford University. In advanced old age his life-long sensitivity to criticism reached an acute state of obsessive overreaction which spoilt much of the media attention he received.

A new generation of poets and writers revered him. To Siegfried Sassoon he was 'the Wessex Wizard'. W.M. Parker, author of the *Letters of Sir Walter Scott*, visited Max Gate in September 1920 and described Hardy as 'the great little Wizard of the South'. Sir James Barrie came in May 1921 and the pair of them walked across the meadows to his Bockhampton birthplace where the writer Hermann Lea had been staying. They found it deserted and locked but Barrie was determined to see inside so they broke in through a window. 'The Fallow Deer at the Lonely House' resulted from another wave of nostalgia.

Hardy's 'favourite walk' from Max Gate, with Wessex, was down Syward Road and across the railway line and the River Frome, then over the meadows to visit the family graves in Stinsford churchyard. Despite a serious kidney malfunction in February 1922 he resumed cycling and visited Kate and Henry in Talbothays Lodge, the villa he had designed for them in West Stafford,

Talbothays Lodge, West Stafford, was designed by Thomas Hardy and built by brother Henry for their sister Kate

making another of his imaginary place-names a real name on the map. He worked on a play, *The Famous Tragedy of the Queen of Cornwall* for his favourite actress, Mrs Gertrude Bugler, and received visits from old friends Florence Henniker and Lady Agnes Grove. Mrs Henniker died in April 1923. The artist Augustus John, living at Poole, captured the image of Hardy with the ageless dignity of a great Victorian.

More than anything else, his lasting reputation in Dorchester was secured by a royal visitor, on 20 July 1923. Edward, Prince of Wales – the future King Edward VIII – called to take him on a tour through the county town which was followed by lunch at Max Gate. The locals were also impressed by regular appearances on a Brough Superior motorcycle of national hero Lawrence of Arabia, Colonel Thomas Edward Lawrence – alias Private Shaw of the Royal Tank Corps–- from Bovington Camp. He 'utterly captivated' Hardy and they

Lawrence of Arabia – subsequently living down the 'Prince of Mecca' image – became a frequent guest at Max Gate

South Dorset's other literary shrine, at Clouds Hill, where Mr and Mrs Hardy visited Lawrence of Arabia

shared a friendship with the author E.M. Forster. Florence and Thomas visited Lawrence's spartan cottage at Clouds Hill which now completes the trio of south Dorset literary properties owned by the National Trust.

Hardy in old age was described by Dorset publisher Sir Newman Flower as:

...a very little man, with a great domed forehead. A very little man with a pricked moustache, and deep-set eyes, a curved nose, and small white hands with stubby fingers. I have never yet seen what I would regard as the perfect photograph of Hardy. But a Russian named [Sergei] Yourievitch made a bust of him in 1924 which has always seemed to me the best portrait. The sculptor beat the camera.

Hardy was less impressed with the bust: 'The Russian has put in the large curved nose without mercy.' A pro-Soviet visitor, in June 1924, was the composer Rutland Broughton who spent a couple of days at Max Gate. Though he persuaded Hardy to allow him to perform a musical version of *The Queen of Cornwall* at Glastonbury Abbey he utterly failed to convert him to communism.

Hardy finally achieved his aim of proving that poetry could be a best-seller, having his revenge over past critics on 20 November 1925. *Human Shows, Far Phantasies*, in a first edition of 5000 copies, sold out within hours. Everyone now wrote glowingly about him. To Leonard Woolf he was 'the spiritual parent' of modern poets. With Leonard, wife Virginia Woolf visited 'the puffy-cheeked cheerful old man' at Max Gate on Sunday 25 July 1926. He was 'dressed in rough grey with a striped tie', his eyes 'now faded and rather watery'. Hardy recalled seeing Virginia in her cradle 'at Hyde Park Place – oh, Gate was it?' Wessex the dog interrupted the discussion on poetry and they discussed various friends, notably Colonel Lawrence.

'I hope he won't commit suicide,' Mrs Hardy said. 'He promised me not to go into the air,' Hardy said, referring to Lawrence having enlisted in the RAF, though as an aircraftman on the ground. 'My husband doesn't like anything to do with the air,' Florence explained, with the dog then needing her attention. It is with obvious relief that Virginia Woolf tells us, 'Wessex went wheezing away'.

Visiting Lady Hester Pinney at Racedown, near Broadwindsor, in 1925 and again when entertaining Mr and Mrs John Galsworthy at Max Gate in 1927, Hardy left a darker abiding memory. He talked in detail about public hangings. There was also a relaxation of his natural reserve and resistance at meeting a wider audience. Having attended John Drinkwater's adaptation of *The Mayor of Casterbridge*, on stage in Weymouth on 20 September 1926, he received a standing ovation. He also laid the foundation stone of the new Dorchester Grammar School – cementing the Thomas Hardye and Thomas Hardy connection, as he put it – on 21 July 1927. Literary locations were confirmed for posterity after young calligrapher and illustrator Heather Child met Hardy. She produced the decorated map which is now displayed in Dorset County Museum.

Two deaths affected him greatly. Agnes Grove died on 7 December 1926. Then, on the 27th, he was parted from his best friend. 'The Famous Dog Wessex – Faithful, unflinching', to quote his gravestone, lies in the pets' cemetery at Max Gate. The rough-haired terrier was born in August 1913 and they had shared 'thousands of afternoons'. Both Lady Grove and Wessex had their commemorative poems – 'Concerning Agnes' and 'Dead Wessex the Dog to the Household'. Hardy's achievement in old age, as biographer Robert Gittings observed, was to go on writing, as prolific and poignant as ever. The impetus, however, was primarily the loss of love 'then all mourning, mourning'.

The stone to 'Famous Dog Wessex' in the pets' cemetery at Max Gate

Hardy's life gradually drew to a close from 11 December 1927, in bed at Max Gate, with Dr Gowring coming through the snow to diagnose 'old age', and Sydney Cockerell and Sir James Barrie preparing to tell the world. He kept it waiting, for a full month, until the evening of 11 January 1928. Cockerell and Barrie then conspired to pressure Florence into thwarting his wishes. Back in

1924, Hardy had written to Stinsford's vicar, Revd Henry Guise Beatson Cowley: 'Yes, regard me as a parishioner certainly. I hope to be still more one when I am in a supine position some day.' Instead they arranged a Westminster Abbey funeral – overruling the combined pleas of Florence, Kate and Henry – with his heart being removed by Dorchester surgeon Edward Weller Mann for Stinsford burial and the body going to London via Woking Crematorium. The compromise was a 'staggering blow' to Kate Hardy, offending as it did against the old country belief that bodies should be buried intact, and even cosmopolitan friends like Edward Clodd found it 'repellent'. Hardy's publisher Sir Daniel Macmillan and his secretary compounded the agony, by sending out invitations to the Abbey service almost at random, turning the occasion into 'a sick horror' for Florence. 'Today the ashes of Hardy lie but a few feet away from Dickens,' Newman Flower reflected. 'Two great writers who met but never spoke.'

He left more than £90,000 – all of it from his writings – which was a fortune for the time. Former domestic servants saw the irony in this and were muttering for years about the meagre household budget, as they catalogued Hardy's miserly idiosyncrasies, such as removing coal from the fire for future use.

Memorials followed, including that in Poet's Corner, and a stained-glass window in Stinsford church. Augustus John offered his vision of Tess, as a sculpture, but that was turned down. Sydney Cockerell wanted a second Hardy Monument, on the heath behind his birthplace, but American book collector A.E. Newton beat him to it with a 10-feet granite column in the style of a war memorial. It was placed rather incongruously under the beech trees between Hardy's Cottage and his favourite Snail Creep path. John Livingston Lowes unveiled it on behalf of the 'American friends'.

Somewhat better, peering westwards from Colliton Walk at Top o' Town, Dorchester, is Eric Kennington's bronze statue of a seated Hardy. It was unveiled by Sir James Barrie on 2 September 1931 with a speech of characteristic puckishness that dismayed Florence: 'There were years when I thought

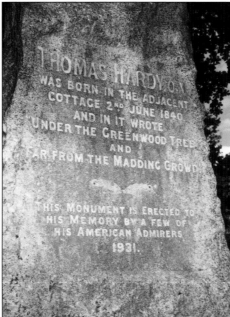

Above left: *His heart in Wessex, shaded by a yew tree, in Stinsford churchyard*

Above middle: *The author's first memorial was a granite oblelisk erected beside Hardy's Cottage by 'a few of his American admirers' in 1931*

Above: *Sundial commemorating Hardy's years at Max Gate (1885 to 1928), added after his death*

Eric Kennington's statue looks westwards from Top o' Town at Dorchester

him the most unhappy man I had ever known.' It was true but hardly appropriate or adequate for the occasion of revealing his lasting likeness to a cynical world. A contemporary comment summed it up: 'Criticism must be withheld, as it doubtless pleased the committee and subscribers who were responsible for its erection.'

Above: *Altar, pulpit and box-pews in the simple single-cell church at Winterborne Tomson*
Above right: *Derelict at the time of his death, the ancient church at Winterborne Tomson was restored in Hardy's memory*

The Society for the Preservation of Ancient Buildings, through its former secretary Albert Reginald Powys – brother of the literary trio John Cowper, Theodore and Llewelyn – sold some Hardy papers and used the cash to restore Winterborne Tomson church in his memory. Hardy wrote that this simple little building, near Bere Regis, had been left 'just as it was when the parishioners went out of it fifty years ago after the last service'.

Florence without Thomas must have seemed a lost soul as she fought rearguard battles against those who had belittled his reputation. More constructively she now enjoyed perfect relations with brother-in-law Henry until he followed Thomas on 9 December 1928. In the new decade, Florence

THE OLD MILL

Recorded as a corn mill in
Domesday 1086 · Granted by
King John to Bindon Abbey
by 1211 · Added to with a
tucking mill in 1310 · Rebuilt
by William & John Churchill
in 1590 and 1602

Rebuilt again as
two corn mills by 1844 and
supplemented with steam
power in 1895 · Remodelled
by the Mill Street Housing
Society in 1940 · Added to
& again remodelled in 1986

Do Well to All Men

Opened by
Richard Best of Godmanstone
Director of
The National Federation of
Housing Associations
11 December 1987

SUSAN WILLIAMS (CHURCHILL)
President
JOHN STARK & PARTNERS · ARCHITECTS

played a leading role in removing the slums from Mixen Lane, as her husband called it, replacing them with modern flats through Mill Street Housing Society. Prime Minister Ramsay MacDonald visited her and discussed the project. Her companions now were her French bulldogs, with Toby being succeeded by Tobina. Florence had suffered various ear, nose and throat problems for years and succumbed to an unrelated cancer on 17 October 1937.

Only Kate was left. A cousin, Nathaniel Sparks (died 1961) – an artist and engraver from Puddletown whose principal work is in Bristol City Museum and Art Gallery – cared for her in advanced old age. She rounded off the Hardy story by seeing his study reconstructed inside Dorset County Museum at Dorchester and had ensured that Max Gate passed to the National Trust with sufficient additional funds for the purchase of the Bockhampton birthplace in 1948. A second acre was added to the garden of Hardy's Cottage by the National Trust in 1967. East of Max Gate, now separated from it by the A35 bypass, the Trumpet Major public house was opened by ex-Prime Minister, and head of Hardy's publishers, Harold Macmillan, as part of the Thomas Hardy Festival on 9 July 1968.

Kate died during the Battle of Britain on 4 October 1940. Overshadowed by events it was the centenary of Hardy's birth and another ex-Premier, Lord Baldwin, laid the commemorative wreath in Dorchester during that first summer of the Second World War. Having returned home from eulogistic speeches a year before, Kate left us this enigmatic thought: 'If they only knew!'

Thomas Hardy's study from Max Gate, complete with furniture and books, was reassembled in Dorset County Museum

GAZETTEER OF HARDY LOCATIONS

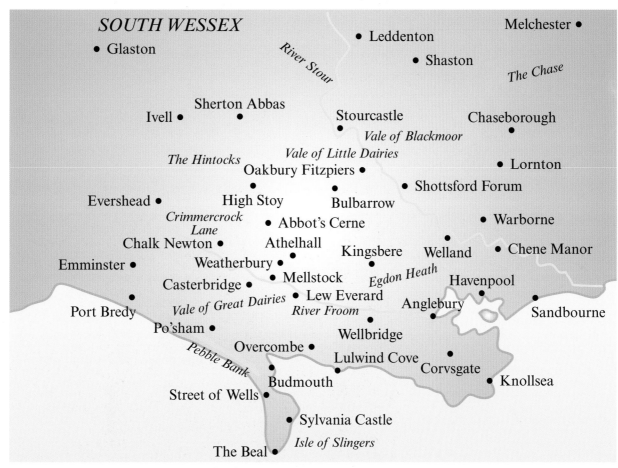

SOUTH WESSEX

- Glaston
- Leddenton
- Melchester
- Shaston
River Stour
The Chase

- Ivell
- Sherton Abbas
- Stourcastle
- Chaseborough
Vale of Blackmoor

Vale of Little Dairies

The Hintocks
- Oakbury Fitzpiers
- Lornton

- Evershead
- High Stoy
- Shottsford Forum
- Bulbarrow
- Warborne

Crimmercrock Lane
- Abbot's Cerne
- Chalk Newton
- Athelhall
- Kingsbere
- Welland
- Chene Manor

- Emminster
- Weatherbury
- Mellstock
Egdon Heath
- Havenpool

- Casterbridge
- Lew Everard
- Anglebury
- Sandbourne

Vale of Great Dairies
River Froom

- Port Bredy
- Po'sham
- Wellbridge

- Overcombe
- Lulwind Cove
- Corvsgate
- Knollsea
Pebble Bank

- Budmouth
- Street of Wells

- Sylvania Castle
Isle of Slingers
- The Beal

Map showing Hardy's Dorset

Hardy's location	Real location
Abbot's Cernel	Cerne Abbas, Dorset
Abbotsea	Abbotsbury, Dorset
Aldbrickham	Reading, Berkshire
Alderworth	Briantspuddle, Dorset
Alfredston	Wantage, Berkshire
Ancient West Highway	Roman road from Winterbourne Abbas to Eggardon Hill, west Dorset
Anglebury	Wareham, Dorset
Anglebury Heath	Northport Heath and Great Ovens Hill, Wareham, Dorset
Antelope Hotel, Casterbridge	itself, Antelope Hotel (now a shopping precinct), Dorchester, Dorset
Antelope Inn, Nuttlebury	itself, Antelope Inn, Hazelbury Bryan, Dorset
Aquae Sulis	itself, being the Roman name for Bath, Somerset
Arrowthorne Lodge	Minstead Lodge, near Lyndhurst, Hampshire
Athelhall	Athelhampton Hall, near Puddletown, Dorset

∽

Back Street, Casterbridge	Trinity Street, Dorchester, Dorset
Baden	itself, the Grand-Duchy of Baden, in Germany
Badger's Clump	Chydyok Farm, Chaldon Herring, Dorset
Bank Walks	itself, Bank Walk between Lower Bockhampton and Stinsford, Dorset
Barnes's Lane	itself, Barnes's Lane bridleway between Alton Pancras and Buckland Newton, Dorset
Barrow Beacon	Beacon Hill, Puddletown, Dorset

Barwith Strand	Trebarwith Strand, near Tintagel, Cornwall
Batten Castle	Lulworth Castle, East Lulworth, Dorset
Bath	itself, Bath, Somerset
Beal Lantern	pre-1905 Portland Bill Lighthouse, now the Bird Observatory, Portland, Dorset
Bede's Inn, London	Clement's Inn, London WC2
Beersheba, Christminster	Jericho district of inner-city Oxford
Belvidere Hotel, Budmouth	itself, Belvedere Private Hotel (now The Sands Hotel), 117–118 The Esplanade, Weymouth, Dorset
Benvill Lane	itself, Benville Lane, near Evershot, Dorset
Biblioll College, Christminster	Balliol College, Oxford
Bimport Street, Shaston	itself, Bimport, Shaftesbury, Dorset
Birthplace	itself, Hardy's Cottage, Veterans' Alley (now Cherry Lane), Higher Bockhampton, Stinsford, Dorset
Black Bull Hotel, Port Bredy	Bull Hotel, East Street, Bridport, Dorset
Black'on	itself, Black Down (with Admiral Hardy's Monument), Portesham, Dorset
Blackmoor Vale	itself, though now generally spelt Blackmore Vale, across north Dorset
Blooms-End	Bhompston Farm, between Lower Bockhampton and Norris Mill, Stinsford, Dorset
Bossiney	itself, Bossiney, near Boscastle, Cornwall
Bowling Walk, Casterbridge	Bowling Alley Walk, Dorchester
Bramshurst Manor	Moyles Court (now Moyles Court School), near Ringwood, Hampshire
Bredy Knap	itself, Bredy Knap (on the A35) above Long Bredy, Dorset

Broad Sidlinch	Sydling St Nicholas, Dorset
Brown House	Red House, between Fawley and Wantage, Berkshire
Bubb-Down	itself, Bubb Down Hill, Melbury Bubb, Dorset
Buckbury Fitzpiers	Okeford Fitzpaine (renamed Oakbury Fitzpiers for the later novels), Dorset
Budmouth	Weymouth, Dorset
Budmouth Barracks	Red Barracks (now Wellington Court), Barrack Road, Weymouth, Dorset
Budmouth Custom House	itself, the Custom House, Custom House Quay, Weymouth, Dorset
Budmouth Regis	Melcombe Regis, Weymouth, Dorset
Bulbarrow	itself, Bulbarrow Hill, central Dorset
Bull Stake Square, Casterbridge	itself, Bull Stake Square (now known as North Square), Dorchester, Dorset

⌇

Camelot	Cadbury Castle, South Cadbury, Somerset
Camelton	Camelford, Cornwall
Cardinal College, Christminster	Christ Church College, Oxford
Cardinal Street, Christminster	St Aldate's Street, Oxford
Carriford	West Stafford, Dorset
Carriford Road	Crossways, Dorset
Carriford Road Station	Moreton Station, near Crossways, Dorset
Casterbridge	Dorchester, Dorset
Casterbridge Barracks	former Marabout Barracks, Poundbury Road, Dorchester, Dorset

Casterbridge Gaol	Dorchester Prison, North Square, Dorchester, Dorset
Casterbridge Grammar School	former Dorchester Grammar School, South Street, Dorchester, Dorset
Casterbridge Museum	Dorset County Museum, High West Street, Dorchester, Dorset
Casterbridge Station	Dorchester (South) Station, Dorchester, Dorset
Casterbridge Workhouse	former Dorchester Union Workhouse, Damer's Road (facing junction with Maud Road), Dorchester, Dorset
Castle Boterel	Boscastle, Cornwall
Castle Inn	itself, Castle Inn (demolished in the 1920s), 7 Middle Street, Yeovil, Somerset
Castle Royal	Windsor Castle, Berkshire
Catknoll Street	Chetnole, Dorset
Chaldon	itself, West Chaldon, near Lulworth, Dorset
Chaldon Down	itself, above West Chaldon and East Chaldon, near Lulworth, Dorset
Chalk Newton	Maiden Newton, Dorset
Chalk Walk, Casterbridge	Colliton Walk, Dorchester, Dorset
Charmley	Charminster, Dorset
Chaseborough	Cranborne, Dorset
Chasetown	alternative for Cranborne, Dorset
Chateau Ringdale	house at Allington, Bridport, moved by Hardy to Harbour Road, West Bay, Bridport, Dorset
Cheltenham	itself, Cheltenham, Gloucestershire
Chene Manor	Canford Manor (now Canford School), near Wimborne, Dorset

Chesil Bank	itself, Chesil Beach, between Abbotsbury and Portland, Dorset
Chief Street, Christminster	High Street, Oxford
Chillington Wood	Killerton Gardens, Broadclyst, near Exeter, Devon
Christminster	Oxford
Church 'with the Italian porch', Christminster	St Mary the Virgin, Oxford
Cirque of the Gladiators, Casterbridge	Maumbury Rings, Dorchester, Dorset
Clammers Gate	itself, Clammers Gate, into Melbury Park from Melbury Osmond, Dorset
Classical Mansion	Wilton House, near Salisbury, Wiltshire
Clavinium	'Clavino' of the Ravenna Cosmography, which Hardy applied to the Roman temple on Jordan Hill, Preston, near Weymouth, Dorset
Cliff 'without a name'	Beeny Cliff, Boscastle, Cornwall
Cliff Martin	Combe Martin, Devon
Clifton Horseleigh	Clifton Maybank, near Sherborne, Dorset
The Close, Melchester	itself, The Close, Salisbury, Wiltshire
Cloton	Chedington or Clapton, west of Corscombe, in the Dorset-Somerset borderlands
Clyffe Hill Clump	itself, Clyffe Hill Clump, Tincleton, Dorset
Conquer Barrow	itself, Conquer Barrow, behind Casterbridge Road (near Max Gate), Dorchester, Dorset
Coomb Barn	itself, Coombe Barn, south-west of Puddletown, Dorset
Coomb Ewelease	sheep pasture on White Hill, Puddletown, Dorset
Corn Street, Casterbridge	South Street and Cornhill, Dorchester, Dorset

Corvsgate	village of Corfe Castle, Dorset
Corvsgate Castle	castle at Corfe Castle, Dorset
Court House, Casterbridge	Shire Hall, High West Street, Dorchester, Dorset
Cresscombe	Letcombe Bassett, near Wantage, Oxfordshire
Creston	Preston, near Weymouth, Dorset
Crimmercrock Lane	Cromlech Crock Road (now the A356), across Toller Down, near Maiden Newton, Dorset
Cross-in-Hand	Cross and Hand wayside stone, near Batcombe, Dorset
Crossy Hand	also the Cross and Hand, near Batcombe, Dorset
Crown Hotel, Shottsford Forum	itself, Crown Hotel, Blandford Forum, Dorset
Crozier College, Christminster	Oriel College, Oxford
Crozier Hotel, Christminster	Mitre Hotel, Oxford
Cuckoo Lane, Mellstock	itself, Cuckoo Lane (south from A35), Higher Bockhampton, Stinsford, Dorset

の

Dagger's Grave	Daggers Gate, near Newland Farm, West Lulworth, Dorset
de Stancy Castle	Dunster Castle, Dunster, Somerset
Deadman's Bay	Chesil Cove, Portland, and Lyme Bay, Dorset
Deansleigh Park	Broadlands House, near Romsey, Hampshire
Delborough	East Chelborough, near Evershot, Dorset
Devil's Bellows	Culpepper's Dish, near Briantspuddle, Dorset
Devil's Door	Devil's Den, Clatford Bottom, Fyfield, Marlborough, Wiltshire

Devil's Kitchen	itself, Devil's Kitchen, on the northern slope of High Stoy, Minterne Magna, Dorset
Dogbury Hill	itself, Dogbury Hill, Minterne Magna, Dorset
Dole Hill	itself, Dole's Hill, Piddlehinton, Dorset
Downstaple	Barnstaple, Devon
Dree-armed Cross	three-armed hand-post at road junction west of Stafford House, West Stafford, Dorset
Duke's Arms, Shaston	Grosvenor Hotel (family name of the Duke of Westminster), Shaftesbury, Dorset
Duncliffe Hill	itself, Duncliffe Hill, near Stour Provost, Dorset
Dundagel	Tintagel, Cornwall
Durnover	Fordington, Dorchester, Dorset
Durnover Great Field	Fordington Field, Dorchester, Dorset
Durnover Green	The Green, Fordington, Dorchester, Dorset
Durnover Hill	Fordington Hill, Dorchester, Dorset
Durnover Hole	weir-pool on River Frome, downstream from Grey's Bridge, Dorchester, Dorset
Durnover Lea	water-meadows at Fordington, Dorchester, Dorset
Durnover Mill	East Mills, Mill Street, Fordington, Dorchester, Dorset
Durnover Moor	water-meadows north of the River Frome, in Stinsford parish, near Dorchester, Dorset

෴

Earl of Wessex Hotel, Sherton Abbas	itself, Crown Hotel, Blandford Forum, Dorset (now the Digby dormitories of Sherborne School
East Egdon	Affpuddle and Briantspuddle, Dorset
East Endelstow	Lesnewth, near Boscastle, Cornwall

East Mellstock	Lower Bockhampton, Stinsford, Dorset
East Quarriers	Grove Cliff group of quarries (namely France, High Headlands, Broadcroft, Yeolands and Silklake Quarries), Portland, Dorset
Eastern village	Easton, Portland, Dorset
Egdon Heath	heathland from Stinsford eastwards to Turners Puddle, Dorset
Eggar	Eggardon Hill, near Askerswell, Dorset
Elensford	Duddle Farm, near Stinsford (though just inside 'the adjoining parish' of Puddletown), Dorset
Elm Cranlynch	Corfe Mullen, Dorset
Emminster	Beaminster, Dorset
Endelstow	St Juliot, near Boscastle, Cornwall
Endelstow House	house in the valley of the River Valency, near Boscastle, Cornwall
Enkworth Court	Encombe House, Kingston, near Corfe Castle, Dorset
Evershead	Evershot, Dorset
Exonbury	Exeter, Devon
Falcon Hotel	White Hart Hotel, Launceston, Cornwall
Falmouth	itself, Falmouth, Cornwall
Falls Park	Mells Park, near Frome, Somerset
The Fane	Temple-style gazebo near the lake, Kingston Maurward, near Stinsford, Dorset
Farnfield	Farnborough, Hampshire
Fensworth	village near Fawley, Berkshire

Fernell Hall	Embley House (now Embley Park School), near Romsey, Hampshire
Field of tombs, Casterbridge	Dorchester Cemetery, Weymouth Road, Dorchester, Dorset
Flintcombe Ash	Barcombe Farm, Alton Pancras, or Plush, near Piddletrenthide, Dorset
Flower-de-Luce, Chaseborough	Fleur-de-Lis, Cranborne, Dorset
Flychett	Lytchett Minster, near Poole, Dorset
Forest of the White Hart	King's Stag, near Lydlinch, Dorset
Forum	Blandford Forum, Dorset
Fountall	Wells, Somerset
Fountall Cathedral	Wells Cathedral, Wells, Somerset
Fountall Theological College	Wells Theological College, Wells, Somerset
Fourways, Christminster	Carfax (a corruption of the French for crossroads), Oxford
Froom	River Frome (pronounced Froom), Dorset
Froom Everard	West Stafford, Dorset
Froom Everard House	Stafford House, West Stafford, Dorset
Froom River	River Frome, Dorset
Frome Side Vale	Frome Valley, Dorset

∽

Gaymead	Shinfield, near Reading, Berkshire
Giant's Town	Hugh Town, St Mary's, Isles of Scilly
Glaston	itself, Glaston being the milestone contraction for Glastonbury, Somerset

Gloucester Lodge, Budmouth	itself, now Gloucester Hotel, Gloucester Row, 85 The Esplanade, Weymouth, Dorset
Great Forest	New Forest, Hampshire
Great Grey Plain	Salisbury Plain, Wiltshire
Great Hintock	Minterne Magna, Dorset
Great Hintock House	Minterne House, Minterne Magna, Dorset
Great Mid-Wessex Plain	Salisbury Plain, Wiltshire
Great Plain	also Salisbury Plain, Wiltshire
Great Pool	weir on the River Frome, Woodsford, Dorset
Green Hill, Kingsbere	Woodbury Hill, Bere Regis, Dorset
Green Hill Fair, Kingsbere	Woodbury Hill Fair, Bere Regis, Dorset
Grey's Bridge, Casterbridge	itself, Grey's Bridge, Dorchester, Dorset
Grey's Wood	itself, Grey's Wood, Higher Kingston, near Stinsford, Dorset

∽

Haggardon Hill	Eggardon Hill, near Askerswell, Dorset
Hangman's Cottage, Casterbridge	itself, Hangman's Cottage, Glyde Path Road, Dorchester, Dorset
Havenpool	Poole, Dorset
Heedless William's Pond	itself, Heedless William's Pond, beside Duddle Heath, near Stinsford, Dorset
Hendford Hill	itself, Hendford Hill, Yeovil, Somerset
Henry the Eighth's Castle	Sandsfoot Castle, Weymouth, Dorset
Heymere House	Clevedon Court, Clevedon, Somerset
High Place Hall, Casterbridge	Colliton House, Glyde Path Road, Dorchester, Dorset

High-Stoy Hill	itself, High Stoy Hill, Minterne Magna, Dorset
High Street, Casterbridge	High West Street, Dorchester, Dorset
Higher Crowstairs	Waterston Ridge, near Puddletown, Dorset
Hintock	a Hardy name that has moved from fiction into fact, being adopted for a telephone exchange covering the southern Blackmore Vale, Dorset
Hintock House	Turnworth House, Turnworth, Dorset
Hintocks	countryside around Bubb Down Hill and High Stoy between Melbury Osmond and Minterne Magna, Dorset
Hocbridge	amalgam of Hoccum and Stourbridge, for a town in the West Midlands
Holway	itself, Holway Lane, from Cattistock to Evershot, Dorset
Holloway Lane	also Holway Lane, from Cattistock to Evershot, Dorset
Holmstoke	amalgam of East Stoke and East Holme, Dorset
Holworth	itself, Holworth, near Owermoigne, Dorset
Hope Church	St Andrew's Church, Church Ope Cove, Portland, Dorset

༄

Icen Way	Roman road across Puddletown Heath, near Puddletown, Dorset
Icenway House	Hackwood House, Winslade, near Basingstoke, Hampshire
Idmouth	Sidmouth, Devon
Ikling Way	Ackling Dyke Roman road, to Salisbury and London, from Badbury Rings, Shapwick, Dorset
Inkpen	Inkpen Beacon, near Newbury, Berkshire

Inner Wessex	Dorset
The Island	Isle of Wight, Hampshire
Isles of Lyonesse	Scilly Isles, Cornwall
Isle of Slingers	Portland, Dorset
Ivel Way	Long Ash Lane (now the A37), from Dorchester and Stratton, Dorset, to Yeovil, Somerset
Ivelchester	Ilchester, Somerset
Ivell	Yeovil, Somerset

ℇ

Jersey	itself, Jersey
Jordon Grove	itself, the Jordan Valley, Preston, near Weymouth

ℇ

Kennetbridge	Newbury (on the River Kennet), Berkshire
King's Arms Inn, Casterbridge	itself, King's Arms Hotel, High East Street, Dorchester, Dorset
King's Hintock Court	Melbury House, Melbury Sampford, Dorset
Kingsbere	Bere Regis, Dorset
Kingsbere Hill	Black Hill, Bere Regis, Dorset
Kingsbere-sub-Greenhill	Bere Regis (beneath Woodbury Hill), Dorset
Knapwater House	Kingston Maurward House, Stinsford, Dorset
Knollingwood Hall	St Giles House, Wimborne St Giles, Dorset
Knollsea	Swanage, Dorset

ℇ

Lambing Corner	itself, Lambing Corner between Caltford and Fyfield, near Marlborough, Wiltshire

Lane Inn, Stagfoot Lane	old Fox Inn, corner of Hartfoot Lane and Cothayes Drove, Lower Ansty, Dorset
Leddenton	Gillingham, Dorset
Lewgate	Higher Bockhampton, near Stinsford, Dorset
Little Enkworth	Kingston, near Corfe Castle, Dorset
Little Hintock	Stockwood and Hermitage, Dorset
Little Weatherbury Farm	Druce Farm, near Puddletown, Dorset
Little Welland	Winterborne Zelston, Dorset
London	itself, London
Long-Ash Lane	itself, Long Ash Lane (now the A37), Dorset
Longpuddle	Piddletrenthide, Dorset
Lord Quantock Arms, Markton	The Luttrell Arms, Dunster, Somerset
Lord's Barrow	itself, Lord's Barrow, West Chaldon, near Lulworth, Dorset
Lornton Inn	Horton Inn, near Horton, Dorset
Lower Longpuddle	Piddlehinton, Dorset
Lower Mellstock	Lower Bockhampton, near Stinsford, Dorset
Lower Wessex	Devon
Lulstead	West Lulworth, Dorset
Lulstead Cove	Lulworth Cove, West Lulworth, Dorset
Lulwind Cove	also Lulworth Cove, West Lulworth, Dorset
Lumsdon	Cumnor, near Oxford
Lydden Spring	itself, the source of the River Lydden, Buckland Newton, Dorset
(Isles of) Lyonesse	Scilly Isles, Cornwall

∽

Mai Dun	Maiden Castle, near Dorchester, Dorset
Maidon	also Maiden Castle, near Dorchester, Dorset
Manor Court	Rushmore House, Tollard Royal, Wiltshire
Market House, Casterbridge	Corn Exchange, North Square, Dorchester, Dorset
Markton	Dunster, Somerset
Marlbury	Marlborough, Wiltshire
Marlbury Downs	Marlborough Downs, Wiltshire
Marshcombe Bottom	Middlemarsh, Minterne Magna, Dorset
Marlott	Marnhull, Dorset
Marshall's Elm	itself, Marshall's Elm, near Street, Somerset
Marshwood	Middlemarsh, near Minterne Magna, Dorset
Martock Moor	itself, being the Somerset Levels near Martock, Somerset
Marygreen	Fawley, Berkshire
Max Gate	itself, Max Gate (originally Mack's Gate), Alington Avenue, Dorchester, Dorset
Melchester	Salisbury, Wiltshire
Melchester Cathedral	Salisbury Cathedral, Wiltshire
Mellstock	Stinsford, Dorset
Mellstock Cross	Stinsford Cross (between Lower Bockhampton and Higher Bockhampton), Stinsford, Dorset
Mellstock Lane	road east from Stinsford Hill to Stinsford Cross and Tincleton, Dorset
Mellstock Leaze	meadows (the Saxon word), south of Church Lane, Stinsford, Dorset

Mellstock Rise	Stinsford Hill (now with a roundabout on the A35), Stinsford, Dorset
Mid Wessex	Wiltshire
Middleton	Milton Abbas, Dorset
Middleton Abbey	Milton Abbey, Milton Abbas, Dorset
Millpond St Jude's	Milborne St Andrew, Dorset
Milton Wood	woods around Delcombe Bottom, Milton Abbas, Dorset
Mistover	Puddletown Heath, Puddletown, Dorset
Mistover Knap	Green Hill, south of Puddletown Beacon, Puddletown, Dorset
Mixen Lane, Durnover	Mill Street, Fordington, Dorset
Montislope	Montacute, Somerset
Moreford	Moreton, Dorset
Moreford Rise	Broomhill, Winfrith Newburgh, Dorset
Mount Lodge	Killerton House, Broadclyst, near Exeter, Devon

༄

Narrobourne	West Coker, near Yeovil, Somerset
Nest Cottage	Chine Hill Cottage (since demolished), Druce, near Puddletown, Dorset
Nether Moynton	Owermoigne, Dorset
Nether Wessex	Somerset
New Castle	Pennsylvania Castle (now Pennsylvania Castle Hotel), Wakeham, Dorset
Nettlecombe Tout	itself, Nettlecombe Tout, Melcombe Horsey, Dorset
Newland Buckton	Buckland Newton, Dorset

Newton	Maiden Newton, Dorset
Nicholas Cottage	itself, St Nicholas Cottage, East Chaldon, Chaldon Herring, Dorset
Norcombe	Burnt Bottom and Westcombe Coppice, Hooke, Dorset
Norcombe Hill	Winyard's Gap, Chedington, Dorset
North Wessex	Berkshire (particularly the part transferred to Oxfordshire in 1974)
North-West Avenue, Casterbridge	The Grove, Dorchester, Dorset
The Nothe, Budmouth	itself, The Nothe, Weymouth, Dorset
Nuttlebury	Hazelbury Bryan, Dorset
Nuzzlebury	also Hazelbury Bryan, Dorset

ॐ

Oakbury Fitzpiers	Okeford Fitzpaine, Dorset
Octagonal Chamber, Christminster	Cupola of the Sheldonian Theatre, Oxford
Off-Wessex	Cornwall
Old Greyhound Inn, Casterbridge	itself, now Old Greyhound Yard, Dorchester, Dorset
Old Harry Rock(s)	itself, at Studland, Dorset
Old Melchester	Old Sarum, near Salisbury, Whiltshire
Old Rooms Inn, Budmouth	itself, the Old Rooms, Trinity Street, Weymouth, Dorset
Old Time Street, Christminster	Oriel Lane, Oxford
Oldgate College, Christminster	New College, Oxford
Oozewood	Ringwood, Hampshire
Oriel Window, Casterbridge	building in High West Street (replaced by the Buzz Inn), Dorchester, Dorset

Outer Wessex	Somerset
Overcombe	Sutton Poyntz, near Weymouth, Dorset (though the actual mill buildings are based on Upwey Mill)
Oxwell	Poxwell, Dorset
Oxwell Hall	Poxwell House, Poxwell, Dorset

∽

Peakhill Cottage	Manor Gardens Cottage, Lower Bockhampton, near Stinsford, Dorset
Pebble Bank	Chesil Beach, from Abbotsbury to Portland, Dorset
Pen-zephyr	Penzance, Cornwall
Peter's Finger, Durnover	former King's Head, Mill Street, Fordington, Dorchester, Dorset
Phoenix Inn, Casterbridge	itself, now Phoenix Court, High East Street, Dorchester, Dorset
Pilsdon	itself, being Pilsdon Pen, as the highest hill in Dorset
Port Bredy	Bridport, Dorset
Port Bredy Harbour	Bridport Harbour, West Bay, Dorset
Pos'ham	itself, being how the locals pronounce Portesham, Dorset
Priory Mill, Casterbridge	former Friary Mill, Friary Hill, Dorchester
Prospect Hotel	Hunter's Inn, Parracombe, near Coombe Martin, Devon
Puddle-sub-Mixen	Turners Puddle, Dorset
Pummery, Casterbridge	itself, being the former local name for Poundbury, Dorchester, Dorset
Pummery Tout, Casterbridge	Poundbury Camp, Poundbury, Dorchester, Dorset
Pure Drop Inn, Marlott	Crown Inn, Marnhull

Pydel Vale	Piddle Valley, upstream of Puddletown, Dorset

〜

Quartershot	Aldershot Camp, Aldershot, Hampshire
Quiet Woman Inn	former Wild Duck Inn (now Duck Dairy House), Duddle Heath, near Puddletown, Dorset

〜

Rainbarrow	itself, the prominent mound of the Rainbarrows cluster on Duddle Heath, Dorset
Red King's Castle	Bow and Arrow Castle (also known as Rufus Castle), Church Ope, Portland, Dorset
Revellers' Inn	former Revel's Inn (now Lower Revels Farm), Cosmore, Buckland Newton, Dorset
Ridgeway	Ridgeway Hill, Weymouth
Rimsmoor Pond	itself, Rimsmoor Pond, south of Briantspuddle, Dorset
The Ring, Casterbridge	Maumbury Rings, Dorchester, Dorset
Rings Hill	Weatherbury Castle hill-fort, Milborne St Andrew, Dorset
Rings Hill Speer	Hood Monument, Butleigh, Somerset
Rolliver's Alehouse, Martlott	former Lamb Inn (now Old Lamb House), Walton Elm Cross, Marnhull
Rook's Gate	entrance to Killerton Park, Broadclyst, near Exeter, Devon
Rookington House	Hurn Court (now Heron Court School), Hurn, Dorset
Rookington Park	Hurn Park, Hurn, Dorset
Round Pound	itself, Round Pound, Chaldon Down, near Lulworth, Dorset
Rou'tor Town	Bodmin (below Rough Tor), Cornwall

Roy Town	Troytown, Puddletown, Dorset
Rubdon Hill	Bubb Down Hill, Melbury Bubb, Dorset
Rubric College, Christminster	Brasenose College, Oxford
Rushy Pond	itself, Rushy Pond, Duddle Heath, near Puddletown, Dorset

❦

St Launce's	Launceston, Cornwall
St Maria's	St Mary's, Isles of Scilly
St Mary's, Toneborough	St Mary Magdalene Church, Church Square, Taunton, Somerset
St Peter's Church	itself, St Peter's Church, High West Street, Dorchester, Dorset
St Peter's Finger, Durnover	former King's Head, Mill Street, Fordington, Dorchester, Dorset
St Silas, Christminster	St Barnabas Church (designed by Hardy's architectural associate Sir Arthur Blomfield), Oxford
The Sallows	riverside wood at Stafford House, West Stafford, Dorset
Sandbourne	Bournemouth
Sandbourne Moor	Bourne Bottom, Poole, Dorset
Sarcophagus College, Christminster	Corpus Christi College, Oxford
Scrimpton	Frampton, Dorset
Shadwater	Woodsford, Dorset
Shadwater Weir	weir on the River Frome at Woodsford Farm, Woodsford, Dorset
Shakeforest Towers	Clatford Hall, Fyfield, Marlborough, Wiltshire

Shaston	itself, Shaston, being the milestone contraction for Shaftesbury, Dorset
Sherton Abbas	Sherborne, Dorset
Sherton Abbas Castle	Sherborne (New) Castle, Sherborne, Dorset
Sherton Abbas Park	Sherborne Park, Sherborne, Dorset
Sherton Castle	Sherborne (Old) Castle, Sherborne, Dorset
Sherton Turnpike	West Hill Cottage, between Longburton and Sherborne, Dorset
Shottsford	Blandford, Dorset
Shottsford Forum	also Blandford Forum, Dorset
Sidlinch	Sydling St Nicholas, Dorset
Silverthorn Dairy	Up Exe, between Silverton and Thorverton, Devon
Sleeping Green	Withycombe, Somerset (with the Old King's Arms) or nearby Carhampton (with the Butchers' Arms)
The Slopes	foothills of Cranborne Chase, Dorset
Slopeway Well	Fortuneswell, Portland, Dorset
Slyer's Lane	itself, Slyer's Lane, Coker's Frome, near Stinsford, Dorset
Snail Creep	itself, Snail Creep being the local name for the path from Higher Bockhampton northwards to Grey's Wood, near Stinsford, Dorset
Solentsea	Southsea, Hampshire
South-Avon	River Avon, Wiltshire and Hampshire
South Wessex	Dorset
Southampton	itself, Southampton, Hampshire
Southerton	Stoborough

Sow-and-Acorn, Evershead	Acorn Inn, Evershot
Springham	Warmwell, Dorset
Stagfoot Lane	Hartfoot Lane, from Bingham's Melcombe to Lower Ansty, Dorset
(de) Stancy Castle	Dunster Castle, Dunster, Somerset
Standfast Bridge, Durnover	East Mills Bridge, Mill Lane, Fordington, Dorchester, Dorset
Stapleford	Stalbridge, Dorset
Stapleford Park	Stalbridge Park, Stalbridge, Dorset
Stickleford	Tincleton, Dorset
Stoke Barehills	Basingstoke, Hampshire
Stoke Lane	itself, Stoke Lane, between Mappowder and Stoke Wake, Dorset
Stonehenge	itself, Stonehenge, near Amesbury, Wiltshire
Stourcastle	Sturminster Newton, Dorset
Stourton Tower	Alfred's Tower, Brewham, Somerset
Street of Wells	High Street, Fortuneswell, Portland, Dorset
Sylvania Castle	Pennsylvania Castle (now Pennsylvania Castle Hotel), Wakeham, Portland, Dorset

∽

Talbothays Dairy	Lower Lewell Farm, West Stafford, Dorset
Talbothays Lodge	itself, Talbothays Lodge (designed by Thomas Hardy and built by Henry Hardy for their sister Kate), West Stafford, Dorset
Targan Bay	Pentargon Bay, near Boscastle, Cornwall
Ten Hatches	itself, the former Ten Hatches (now Coker's Frome Weir), on the River Frome near Stinsford, Dorset

Ten Hatches Hole, Casterbridge	itself, below the former Ten Hatches, Coker's Frome, Dorchester, Dorset
Tess's Cottage, Evershead	itself, Tess Cottage, up the hill on the west side of the parish church, Evershot, Dorset
Tess's Cottage, Marlott	Barton Cottage (now Tess Cottage), Walton Elm, Marnhull, Dorset
Tewnell Mill	Hooke Mill, Hooke, near Beaminster, Dorset
Theatre of Wren, Christminster	Sheldonian Theatre, Oxford
Thorncombe Wood, Mellstock	itself, Thorncombe Wood (beside Hardy's Cottage), Higher Bockhampton, near Stinsford, Dorset
Three Mariners' Inn, Casterbridge	itself, the former King of Prussia later known as the Three Mariners, High East Street (standing on the north side, east of Friary Lane), Dorchester, Dorset
Three Tranters' Inn	Wise Man Inn, West Stafford, Dorset
Throope Corner, Alderworth	junction at Throop Clump, Briantspuddle, Dorset
Tintinhull	itself, Tintinhull, near Montacute, Somerset
Tintinhull Valley	itself, at Tintinhull, beside Wellhams Brook below Stoke sub Hamdon, Somerset
Tolchurch	Tolpuddle, Dorset
Toneborough	Taunton (on the River Tone), Somerset
Toneborough Barracks	Jellalabad Barracks, Mount Street, Taunton, Somerset
Toneborough Deane	Vale of Taunton Deane, Somerset
Tor-upon-Sea	Torquay, Devon
Town Bridge, Melchester	St Nicholas Bridge, Salisbury
Trantridge	Pentridge, Dorset
Trufal	itself, Trufal, Cornwall
Tudor College, Christminster	Brazenose College, Oxford

Tutcombe Bottom	Lewcombe, East Chelborough, Dorset
The Union, Casterbridge	itself, the former Union Workhouse, otherwise known as the Poor Law Institution, Damer's Road (facing junction with Maud Road), Dorchester, Dorset

᷍

Uplandtowers	St Giles House, Wimborne St Giles, near Cranborne, Dorset
Upper Longpuddle	Piddletrenthide, Dorset
Upper Mellstock	Higher Bockhampton, near Stinsford, Dorset
Upper Wessex	Hampshire

᷍

Vagg Hollow	itself, Vagg Hollow below Vagg Farm, Vagg, north-west of Yeovil, Somerset
Vale of Blackmoor	itself, though the general spelling is now for the Vale of Blackmore, across north Dorset
Valley of the Little Dairies	Blackmore Vale, Dorset
Valley of the Great Dairies	Frome Valley, Dorset
Vindilia	Portland, Dorset
Vindogladia	Woodyates, near Pentridge, Dorset

᷍

Warborne	Wimborne, Dorset
Warm'ell Cross	itself, Warmwell Cross (now a roundabout), near Warmwell, Dorset
Waterstone Ridge	itself, Waterston Ridge, south of Lacock Dairy Farm, near Puddletown, Dorset
Weatherbury	Puddletown (known as Piddletown in Hardy's time), Dorset

Weatherbury Farm	Waterston Manor, between Piddlehinton and Puddletown, Dorset
Weatherbury Vicarage	itself, the former Vicarage, now Dawney House, Puddletown, Dorset
Welcome Home Inn, Castle Boterel	The Ship, The Harbour, Boscastle, Cornwall
Welland Bottom	Almer, near Sturminster Marshall, Dorset
Welland House	Charborough House, Morden, Dorset
Wellbridge	Wool Bridge, Wool, Dorset
Wellbridge Abbey	Bindon Abbey, Wool, Dorset
Wellbridge House	Woolbridge Manor, Wool, Dorset
Wellbridge Manor	also Woolbridge Manor, Wool, Dorset
Wellbridge Mill	Bindon Mill, Wool, Dorset
Wessex Heights	escarpments of the Dorset Downs and Quantock Hills, plus those of Hampshire Downs and Berkshire Downs
West Endelstow	St Juliot, near Boscastle, Cornwall
West Endelstow Church	St Julietta's Church, St Juliot, near Boscastle, Cornwall
West Poley	Priddy, near Wells, Somerset
West Walk, Casterbridge	West Walks, Dorchester, Dorset
Weydon Fair	Weyhill Fair, near Andover, Hampshire
Weydon Priors	Hurstbourne Priors, near Andover, Hampshire
Wherryborne	Winterborne Came, near Dorchester, Dorset
Wherryborne Rectory	Old Rectory (home of pastor-poet William Barnes), Winterborne Came, near Dorchester, Dorset
Wherryborne Wood	North Plantation, Came Park, Winterborne Came, near Dorchester, Dorset

Whit' Sheet Hill	itself, Whitesheet Hill, where Cromlech Crock Road (now the A356) ascends the downs north of Toller Fratrum, Dorset
White Hart Tavern, Casterbridge	itself, White Hart Hotel, High East Street, Dorchester, Dorset
White Horse Inn, Chalk Newton	itself, the old White Horse Inn, Maiden Newton, Dorset
White-Hart Valley	Blackmore Vale
Windy Beak	Cambeak, St Gennys, near Bude, Cornwall
Wintoncester	Winchester, Hampshire
Wintoncester Cathedral	Winchester Cathedral, Winchester, Hampshire
Wolfeton House	itself, Wolfeton House, Charminster, Dorset
Woolcomb	itself, Woolcombe, near Evershot, Dorset
Wylls Neck	itself, Wills Neck, West Bagborough, Somerset
Wyndway House	Upton House, Poole, Dorset
Wynyard's Gap	itself, Winyard's Gap, near Chedington, Dorset

෴

Yalbury Hill	Yellowham Hill, near Puddletown, Dorset
Yalbury Wood	Yellowham Wood, between Stinsford and Puddletown, Dorset
Yellowham Bottom	itself, the combe on the west side of Yellowham Wood, near Stinsford, Dorset
Yewsholt Lodge	Farr's House, Cowgrove, near Pamphill, Dorset